WORKBOOK

FOR

WHEELOCK'S

LATIN:

AN INTRODUCTORY COURSE

Prepared by

Paul T. Comeau

Department of Foreign Languages

New Mexico State University

BARNES & NOBLE BOOKS

A DIVISION OF HARPER & ROW, PUBLISHERS

New York, Cambridge,

Philadelphia, San Francisco, London,

Mexico City, São Paulo, Sydney

ISBN: 0-06-460192-7
LIBRARY OF CONGRESS CATALOG CARD NUMBER: 79-2753

90   10 9

CONTENTS

PREFACE

This workbook, ancillary to Wheelock's <u>Latin</u>: <u>An Introductory Course</u> <u>Based on Ancient Authors</u>, has been developed especially for high-school and college students and any private-study individuals* who, as a result of a somewhat limited linguistic experience, may desire the extra auxiliary guidance and discipline provided by the written exercises of this book. The student should begin by studying the material in a given chapter of Wheelock's <u>Latin</u> and should then review and strengthen such study by writing out the fill-in exercises on that lesson. Having mastered the text of each chapter, the student will then be well prepared to read with pleasure the <u>Sententiae Antiquae</u>, which are the most important and rewarding part of each chapter (see Wheelock, pp. viii-ix).

Each chapter is organized under the following headings.
1. OBJECTIVES. This section sets forth what the students are expected to accomplish in the study of each chapter.
2. GRAMMAR. Forms and their meanings; usages. Note the admonition in each chapter to Memorize Paradigms (Models) and Vocabularies by Repeating Them Aloud. This method, though admittedly somewhat tedious, is crucial for the successful study of Latin since one can thus learn through the <u>two</u> senses of <u>sight</u> and <u>hearing</u>. (See W.p.1 n.2).
3. DRILL. This provides written practice with individual words, groups of words, and short sentences in order to use the rules and the vocabulary of the chapter and thus to form a sort of transition between the GRAMMAR and the PRACTICE SENTENCES.
4. PRACTICE SENTENCES. These are substantial sentences illustrative of the work of a chapter; but they are not to be regarded as a substitute for the genuine Roman <u>Sententiae</u> <u>Antiquae</u> of each chapter in Wheelock's <u>Latin</u>.

No doubt a person would soon discover that some of the drill material and all the Practice Sentences have been selected from the Optional Self-Tutorial Exercises in Wheelock's <u>Latin</u> and that there is a key for this material. However, as a matter of mature common sense and of one's own practical instruction, one should always write out these exercises for correction independently <u>before</u> ever consulting the key. Consulting the key first would obviously be a complete futility and waste of time. The fill-ins may be corrected in the classroom or however the instructor may decide. Of course, if a person is using the Workbook with Wheelock's <u>Latin</u> as a private or self-paced study project, then the key (where available) may ultimately provide the easiest method for correcting the answers.

My first debt of gratitude is owed to Professor Wheelock for granting permission to use some of his material in this form and for painstakingly reviewing and editing the two preliminary versions of this workbook. The wisdom of his advice and the perceptiveness of his comments have greatly contributed to improving the quality of the workbook. Without his encouragement and support, the project could not have been concluded. Ms. Nancy Cone, Editor of the Barnes and Noble Division of Harper & Row, deserves an

*This category includes students in a self-paced study program and individuals of whatever age who wish to study or review Latin as an independent private project via Wheelock's <u>Latin</u>.

PREFACE

expression of appreciation for her kind help in the publication of the work-book. I am also grateful to Professor Charles Elerick, Department of Linguistics, University of Texas at El Paso and Professor Jacques Laroche, Department of Foreign Languages, New Mexico State University, for having patiently worked with the two preliminary versions in their classrooms during the past two years and for having made many helpful suggestions. I also acknowledge the helpfulness of many courageous students in my class sections since the Fall of 1976 who struggled through the course while the material was being tested. I further express my thanks to the typists, Mrs. Bertha Nava and Mrs. Gloria Lewis, who transformed a difficult manu-script into a finished product of professional quality. Any errors, inaccuracies or misconceptions are mine alone.

P.T.C.

CHAPTER I

The First and Second Conjugations (LAUDŌ, MONEŌ):
Present Infinitive, Indicative and Imperative Active.

OBJECTIVES:

1. To understand the difference between the factors which mark person and number of an English verb tense and those which mark a Latin verb tense.

2. To learn the active voice personal endings of a Latin verb.

3. To learn the present tense of the infinitive, and the indicative and imperative moods, active voice, of the Latin first and second conjugations.

I. GRAMMAR.
   (MEMORIZE PARADIGMS (MODELS) AND VOCABULARY BY REPEATING THEM ALOUD!)

   1. Person and number in an English tense are determined by the

      ....

   2. Person and number in a Latin tense are determined by the

      ....

   3. Write the personal endings for the active voice of a Latin verb and give the English pronoun equivalent to each.

	Singular		Plural
	Latin Ending	English Pronoun(s)	Latin Ending	English Pronoun(s)
1.	...... or .... = ...	1.	.... = ...
2.	.... = ...	2.	.... = ...
3.	.... = ...	3.	.... = ...

   4. The present active infinitive of the Latin verb which means to praise is .... (It will serve as the model verb for the first conjugation throughout the course.)

   5. The present active infinitive of the Latin verb which means to advise is .... (It will serve as the model for the second conjugation throughout the course.)

6. The following forms are .... of Latin verbs.

Give the conjugation to which they belong and their English meaning.

		Conjugation	Meaning
a.	vidēre	....	....
b.	dare	....	....
c.	valēre	....	....
d.	cōgitāre	....	....
e.	dēbēre	....	....
f.	amāre	....	....
g.	servāre	....	....
h.	vocāre	....	....
i.	cōnservāre	....	....
j.	errāre	....	....

7. The present stem is formed by dropping .... from the ....

.... which produces the stem .... for the first

conjugation and .... for the second conjugation.

8. Write the conjugation of DŌ in the present indicative active and the three English present forms which translate it.

		Latin	English Form 1	English Form 2	English Form 3
Singular	1.	....	....	....	....
	2.	....	....	....	....
	3.	....	....	....	....
Plural	1.	....	....	....	....
	2.	....	....	....	....
	3.	....	....	....	....

9. Write the conjugation of DĒBEŌ in the present indicative active and the three English present forms which translate it.

		Latin	English Form 1	English Form 2	English Form 3
Singular	1.	....	....	....	....
	2.	....	....	....	....
	3.	....	....	....	....
Plural	1.	....	....	....	....
	2.	....	....	....	....
	3.	....	....	....	....

10. The model, pattern or example forms for the words of an inflected

language are called ....

CHAPTER I

NAME _____ SECTION _____ DATE _____

II. DRILL.

A. Fill in the following blanks with the information requested.

		Person	Number	Tense	Mood	Voice	Translation
a.	vocā	......	......	.....	....	.....	....
b.	valēte	......	......	.....	....	.....	....
c.	vidēte	......	......	.....	....	.....	....
d.	dā	......	......	.....	....	.....	....
e.	cōgitā	......	......	.....	....	.....	....
f.	cōgitāte	......	......	.....	....	.....	....
g.	valē	......	......	.....	....	.....	....
h.	vidē	......	......	.....	....	.....	....
i.	date	......	......	.....	....	.....	....
j.	vocāte	......	......	.....	....	.....	....

B. Fill in the blanks for each verb:

		Person	Number	Tense	Mood	Voice	Translation
a.	vocat	......	......	.....	....	.....	....
b.	cōgitāmus	......	......	.....	....	.....	....
c.	amant	......	......	.....	....	.....	....
d.	dēbēs	......	......	.....	....	.....	....
e.	videt	......	......	.....	....	.....	....
f.	vident	......	......	.....	....	.....	....
g.	dēbēmus	......	......	.....	....	.....	....
h.	valēs	......	......	.....	....	.....	....
i.	datis	......	......	.....	....	.....	....
j.	amās	......	......	.....	....	.....	....

C. Supply the correct present active indicative form of the verb in parentheses and translate.

a. Saepe .... (Errāre; 2nd person plural)

....

b. .... nihil . (Vidēre; 1st person plural)

....

c. .... mē . (Amāre; 3rd person singular)

....

d. Quid .... ? (Vidēre; 2nd person plural)

....

e. Vocā mē sī .... (Errāre; 3rd person plural)

....

f. .... nihil . (Dare; 2nd person plural)

....

g. Quid .... ? (Servāre; 1st person plural)

....

h. Saepe nihil .... (Dare; 3rd person singular)

....

i. Mē .... (Amāre; 3rd person plural)

....

j. Monē mē sī nihil .... (Vidēre; 2nd person singular)

....

III. PRACTICE SENTENCES. (Before translating each, read the Latin aloud twice.)

a. Monent mē sī errō. ....

b. Monet mē sī errant. ....

c. Monēte mē sī errat. ....

d. Dēbēs monēre mē. ....

e. Dēbētis servāre mē. ....

f. Nōn dēbent laudāre mē. ....

g. "Quid dat?" "Saepe nihil dat." ....

h. Mē saepe vocant et (and) monent. ....

i. Nihil videō. Quid vidēs? .... ?

j. Mē laudā sī nōn errō. ....

k. Sī valētis, valēmus. ....

l. Sī valet, valeō. ....

m. Sī mē amat, dēbet mē laudāre. ....

n. Cōnservāte mē. ....

o. Nōn dēbeō errāre. ....

p. Quid dēbēmus laudāre? .... ?

q. Videt; cōgitat; monet. ....

CHAPTER II

Cases:
First Declension;
Agreement of Adjectives.

OBJECTIVES:

1. To learn each case or form of a Latin noun and the role or function or use of each one in a Latin sentence.

2. To learn the declension and gender of first declension nouns and adjectives.

I. GRAMMAR.
   (MEMORIZE PARADIGMS (MODELS) AND VOCABULARY BY REPEATING THEM ALOUD!)

   1. The Latin expressions for the definite article "the" and the

      indefinite articles "a" or "an" are ....

   2. Name the Latin cases representing each of the following constructions or ideas:

      a. Direct object of a verb ....

      b. Possession ....

      c. Subject of a verb ....

      d. Means ....

      e. Direct address ....

      f. Agent ....

      g. Indirect object of a verb ....

      h. Manner ....

      i. Accompaniment ....

      j. Place ....

   3. Fill in the following blanks with the information requested for each first declension ending.

	Case	Number	Function	English Preposition (if any)
-ās	....	....	....	....
-a	vocative		....	....

	Case	Number	Function	(if any) English Preposition
-am	....	....	....	....
-ae	vocative	....	....	....
-ae	dative	....	....	....
-a	nominative	....	....	....
-ā	....	....	....	....
-īs	ablative	....	....	....
-ae	genitive	....	....	....
-ae	nominative	....	....	....
-īs	dative	....	....	....
-ārum	....	....	....	....

4. Though Latin first declension nouns are normally feminine, three examples of masculine nouns of that declension are:

Latin	English
....	....
....	....
....	....

5. Complete the declension:

Singular	Case	English Meaning
Pecūnia	....	....
....	....	....
....	....	....
....	....	....
....	....	....
....	....	....

Plural	Case	English Meaning
Pecūniae		
....	....	....
....	....	....
....	....	....
....	....	....
....	....	....
....	....	....

6. Fill in the following blanks with the information requested for each noun.

		English Meaning	Use and English Preposition (if any)
a.	fōrmam	....	....
b.	fāma	....	....
c.	fortūnās	....	....
d.	īrae (nominative plural)	....	....
e.	philosophiae (dative singular)	....	....
f.	puellīs	....	....
g.	pecūnia	....	....
h.	vītae (genitive singular)	....	....
i.	poenārum	....	....
j.	patriīs	....	....

CHAPTER II

NAME _____ SECTION _____ DATE _____

II. DRILL. Supply the correct form of the words, shown in parentheses in the nominative case, and translate:

a. .... (puella) cōgitat.

   ....

b. Date .... (pecūnia).

   ....

c. Sine .... (īra) monet.

   ....

d. Vidēmus .... (fōrma; plural).

   ....

e. .... (nauta) dant ....(poena; plural).

   ....

f. Amātis ....(vīta; singular) et .... (puella; plural).

   ....

g. Est sine ....(multa pecūnia; singular).

   ....

h. Nōn servās .... (patria).

   ....

i. ....(fortūna) vocat.

   ....

j. Laudō ....(philosophia antīqua).

   ....

k. Cōnservant tuam philosophiam ....(vīta; genitive).

   ....

l. Fōrma .... (porta, genitive plural) est antīqua.

   ....

III. PRACTICE SENTENCES. (Before translating each, read the Latin <u>aloud</u> twice.)

    a. Valē, patria mea. ....

    b. Fortūna puellae est magna. ....

    c. Puella fortūnam patriae tuae laudat. ....

    ....

    d. Ō puella, patriam tuam servā. ....

    e. Multae puellae pecūniam amant. ....

    f. Puellae nihil datis. ....

    g. Pecūniam puellae videt. ....

    h. Pecūniam puellārum nōn vidēs. ....

    ....

    i. Monēre puellās dēbēmus. ....

    j. Laudāre puellam dēbent. ....

    k. Vīta multīs puellīs fortūnam dat. ....

    ....

    l. Vītam meam pecūniā tuā cōnservās. ....

    ....

    m. Fāma est nihil sine fortūnā. ....

    n. Vītam sine pecūniā nōn amātis. ....

    ....

    o. Sine famā et fortūnā patria nōn valet. ....

    ....

    p. Īram puellārum laudāre nōn dēbēs. ....

    ....

    q. Vītam sine poenīs amāmus. ....

    r. Sine philosophiā nōn valēmus. ....

    s. Quid est vīta sine philosophiā? ....

CHAPTER III

Second Declension:
Masculine Nouns and Adjectives;
Word Order.

OBJECTIVES:

1. To know and understand the implications of the usual order of words in the English sentence and in a Latin sentence.

2. To learn the declension of second declension masculine nouns ending in -US and -ER and second declension masculine adjectives ending in -US.

I. GRAMMAR.
   (MEMORIZE PARADIGMS (MODELS) AND VOCABULARY BY REPEATING THEM ALOUD!)

   1. In English, the order of words in a sentence is (Circle one.)

        crucial   secondary

   2. In Latin, the order of words in a sentence is (Circle one.)

        crucial   secondary

   3. Assign numbers 1-5 to the following to show the typical order of words in a simple Latin sentence or clause:

        .... Subject and its modifiers

        .... Verb

        .... Adverbial words or phrases

        .... Direct object

        .... Indirect object

   4. The typical order listed above reflects the Roman fondness for a style indicating (Circle one.)

        emphasis   suspense   variety

   5. Nouns of the second declension with nominatives ending in -US or -ER are generally (Circle one.)

        masculine   feminine   neuter

6. Give the indicated information for each of the following second
   declension masculine case endings.

	Case	Number	Function	English Preposition(s) (if any)
-ō	ablative	....	....	....
-um	....	....	....	....
-ō	dative	....	....	....
-ī	vocative	....	....	....
-ōrum	....	....	....	....
-us	....	....	....	....
-ōs	....	....	....	....
-ī(sing).	....	....	....	....
-e	....	....	....	....
-īs	ablative	....	....	....
-ī	nominative	....	....	....
-īs	dative	....	....	....

7. Give the indicated information for each of the following:

		Case	Function	Translation
a.	fīliōrum meōrum	....	....	....
b.	fīliō meō	ablative	....	....
c.	populī Rōmānī	genitive	....	....
d.	populō Rōmānō	dative	....	....
e.	virīs Rōmānīs	ablative	....	....
f.	virī magnī	nominative	....	....
g.	virōrum Rōmānōrum	....	....	....
h.	amīcōrum paucōrum	....	....	....
i.	amīcīs meīs	dative	....	....

		Case	Function	Translation
j.	amīcō meō	ablative	....	....
k.	amīcī Rōmānī	vocative	....	....
l.	multīs puerīs	ablative	....	....
m.	magnum virum	....	....	....
n.	puer meus	....	....	....
o.	multōs agrōs	....	....	....
p.	magnī numerī (sing)	....	....	....
q.	numerī meī	nominative	....	....
r.	puerōrum meōrum	....	....	....
s.	populus Rōmānus	....	....	....
t.	amīce magne	....	....	....

CHAPTER III

NAME _____ SECTION _____ DATE _____

II. DRILL.

A. Supply the correct form of the words, shown in parentheses in the nominative case, and translate:

a. Habēmus semper ....(sapientia).

....

b. Numerus ....(puer; genitive plural) errat.

....

c. Dat sapientiam ....(fīlius meus; dative plural).

....

d. Paucī puerī vident ....(numerus magnus; singular)

.... (vir magnus; genitive plural). ....

....

e. Vocāte ....(vir; plural) ....(magna

sapientia; genitive singular). ....

....

B. Translate the following:

a. The wisdom of men is great.

....

b. The people give much money to the sons of Romans.

....

c. My son sees the girl.

....

d. We praise the boy's friends.

....

e. Many men do not love the great wisdom of philosophy.

....

III. PRACTICE SENTENCES.   (Before translating each, read the Latin <u>aloud</u> twice.)

a. Valē, mī amīce. ....

b. Populus Rōmānus sapientiam fīliī tuī laudat. ....

....

c. Ō vir magne, populum Rōmānum servā. ....

....

d. Numerus populī Rōmānī est magnus. ....

....

e. Multī puerī puellās amant. ....

f. Fīliō meō nihil datis. ....

g. Virōs in agrō videō. ....

h. Amīcum fīliī meī vidēs. ....

i. Amīcum fīliōrum tuōrum nōn videt. ....

....

j. Dēbēmus fīliōs meōs monēre. ....

k. Dēbent fīlium tuum laudāre. ....

l. Vīta paucīs virīs fāmam dat. ....

m. Mē in numerō amīcōrum tuōrum habēs. ....

....

n. Virī magnī paucōs amīcōs saepe habent. ....

....

o. Amīcus meus semper cōgitat. ....

p. Fīlius magnī virī nōn semper est magnus vir. ....

....

q. Sapientiam magnōrum virōrum nōn semper vidēmus. ....

....

r. Philosophiam, sapientiam magnōrum virōrum, laudāre dēbētis. ....

....

CHAPTER IV

Neuters of the Second Declension;
Summary of Adjectives;
Present Indicative of SUM;
Predicate Nouns and Adjectives.

OBJECTIVES:

1. To learn the declension of neuter nouns and adjectives of the second declension.

2. To review the complete declension of first/second declension adjectives ending in -US, -A, -UM (masculine, feminine, neuter).

3. To learn the conjugation of the irregular verb ESSE (to be) in the present indicative tense.

4. To learn the function of predicate nouns and adjectives in Latin syntax.

I. GRAMMAR.
   (MEMORIZE PARADIGMS (MODELS) AND VOCABULARY BY REPEATING THEM ALOUD!)

   1. Except in the nominative, accusative and vocative cases, the forms or inflections of the neuter second declension nouns are the same as (Circle one.)

      Declension 1 masculine   Declension 2 masculine   Declension 1 feminine

   2. The first declension contains no nouns of which of the following genders? (Circle one.)

      Masculine   Feminine   Neuter

   3. The two cases which always have the same ending in the neuter gender only are (Circle one.)

      Dative & ablative   Nominative & accusative   Nominative & genitive

   4. Fill in the following blanks with the information requested for each second declension neuter ending:

	Case	Number	Function	English Preposition(s) (if any)
-ōrum	....	....	....	....
-ī	....	....	....	....
-um	accusative	....	....	....

	Case	Number	Function	English Preposition(s) (if any)
-īs	ablative	....	....	....
-ō	ablative	....	....	....
-um	nominative	....	....	....
-a	accusative	....	....	....
-īs	dative	....	....	....
-ō	dative	....	....	....
-a	nominative	....	....	....

5. Adjectives have masculine, feminine and neuter endings so that, in
   addition to agreeing in number and case, they may agree in ....

6. Complete the declension (omit the vocative).

officium	vērum	Case	English Meaning
....	....	....	....
....	....	....	....
....	....	....	....
....	....	....	....
....	....	....	....
....	....	....	....
....	....	....	....
....	....	....	....
....	....	....	....
....	....	....	....

7. Fill in the following blanks with the information requested for each
   noun.

	Translation	Function
a. donōrum	....	....

	Translation	Function
b. cōnsiliī	....	....
c. officiō	....	....
d. perīculīs	....	....
e. bella	....	....

8. The personal endings of ESSE in the present indicative, when compared with the standard active voice personal endings in Latin, are (Circle one.)

               identical   different

9. Since ESSE is an intransitive verb, it serves to connect a subject with another noun or adjective called a (Circle one.)

              direct object   predicate

10. Predicate nouns must always agree with their subject in case and

    number but not always in ....

11. Translate the following:

    a. sumus ....

    b. sunt   ....

    c. sum   ....

    d. estis ....

    e. est   ....

    f. es   ....

CHAPTER IV

NAME _____ SECTION _____ DATE _____

II. DRILL.

A. Translate each of the following into Latin or English.

a. real danger (subject) ....

b. ōtium magnum ....

c. bella mala ....

d. dōna bella ....

e. from a foolish plan ....

f. perīculī vērī ....

g. for great leisure ....

h. an evil war (direct object) ....

i. by beautiful gifts ....

j. cōnsilia stulta ....

k. of small services ....

l. officiō parvō ....

B. Supply the correct forms of the words shown in parentheses in the nominative case and translate.

a. .... (perīculum) sunt ....(vērus, a, um).

....

b. Perīculum ....(bellum, genitive) est ....(parvus, a, um).

....

c. Puer et puella sunt ....(bellus, a, um).

....

d. Officium et ōtium sunt ....(bonus, a, um).

....

e. Videō ....(cūra; plural) et ....(mora; plural).

....

C. Translate the following:

a. War is evil

....

b. Peace is good.

....

c. The teacher loves service.

....

d. Your eyes are pretty.

....

e. The danger of delays is real.

....

III. PRACTICE SENTENCES. (Before translating each, read the Latin aloud twice.)

a. Multa bella ōtium nōn cōnservant. ....

....

b. Et ōtium perīcula saepe habet. ....

....

c. Stultus vir perīcula bellī laudat. ....

....

d. Ōtium bellō saepe nōn cōnservāmus. ....

....

e. Populus Rōmānus ōtium bonum nōn semper habet. ....

....

f. Patriam et ōtium bellīs parvīs saepe servant. ....

....

g. Sine morā cūram officiō dare dēbēmus. ....

....

h. Perīculum est magnum. ....

i. In magnō perīculō sumus. ....

    ....

j. Vīta nōn est sine multīs perīculīs. ....

    ....

k. Amīcus meus est vir magnī officiī. ....

    ....

l. Officia magistrī sunt multa et magna. ....

    ....

m. Vir parvī ōtiī es. ....

n. Virī magnae cūrae estis. ....

o. Sine oculīs vīta est nihil. ....

    ....

CHAPTER V

First and Second Conjugations:
Future Indicative Active;
Adjectives of the First and Second Declension in -ER.

OBJECTIVES:

1. To learn the conjugation of the active future indicative of the Latin first and second conjugations.

2. To learn the declension of the first and second declension adjectives ending in -ER.

I. GRAMMAR.
   (MEMORIZE PARADIGMS (MODELS) AND VOCABULARY BY REPEATING THEM ALOUD!)

   1. The present stems for the first two conjugations studied in Chapter I were obtained by dropping .... from LAUDĀRE and .... from MONĒRE to produce the stems .... and ....

   2. The active indicative future used to indicate future time in the Latin first and second conjugations is composed of three elements in the following order: ...., ..., and ....

   3. Give the PERSONAL ENDINGS only for the following active indicative tenses of the first two conjugations:

	Present		Future	
	Singular	Plural	Singular	Plural
1.	....	....	....	....
2.	....	....	....	....
3.	....	....	....	....

4. Give the FUTURE TENSE SIGN only for the first two conjugations:

<u>First</u>   <u>Second</u>

Singular   Plural   Singular   Plural

1. .... | 1. ....

2. .... | 2. ....

3. .... | 3. ....

5. Write the conjugation of the active indicative future in Latin and
    English of the following:

<u>Vocāre</u>   <u>To call</u>   <u>Habēre</u>   <u>To have</u>

1. .... | ....

Singular 2. .... | ....

3. .... | ....

1. .... | ....

Plural 2. .... | ....

3. .... | ....

6. When we studied second declension Latin nouns ending in -ER like AGER
    and PUER, we discovered that the only way to tell whether the E
    remained or was dropped was to memorize the Genitive form; and we also
    discovered that the genitive provides the stem for the other cases,
    i.e. AGRĪ and PUERĪ. Adjectives of Declension 1/2 with a masculine
    -ER ending include some which retain and some which drop the E. What
    forms of these adjectives must be memorized to detect the stem for the
    other cases?

    ....

7. Decline the following adjectives:

<u>Singular</u>

Nom	līber	lībera	līberum	noster	nostra	nostrum
Gen	....	....	....	....	....	....
Dat	....	....	....	....	....	....
Acc	....	....	....	....	....	....
Abl	....	....	....	....	....	....

Plural

Nom .... |..........   ....

Gen .... |..........   ....

Dat .... |...........   ....

Acc .... |...........   ....

Abl .... |...........   ....

CHAPTER V

NAME _____ SECTION _____ DATE _____

II. DRILL.

A. Translate the following into English or Latin.

a. amābimus ....

b. valēbit ....

c. vidēbunt ....

d. superābimus ....

e. cogitābō ....

f. I shall have ....

g. You (plural) will have ....

h. She will err ....

i. We shall give ....

j. They will remain ....

B. Supply the correct forms of the words shown in parentheses and translate.

a. Animī (plural) ....(superāre; future).

....

b. ....(superāre, 1st person plural, future) perīcula.

....

c. Sapientia satis .... (valēre; future).

....

d. ....(dare, 2nd person plural, future) glōriam amīcō.

....

e. Tum culpa nostra ....(remanēre; future).

....

f. Puella et puer ....(errāre; future).

....

g. ....(vidēre, 1st person singular, future) magistrōs.

....

h. Morae et cūrae ....(remanēre; future).

....

i. ....(cōgitāre, 2nd person singular, future) dē

philosophiā.

....

j. Propter bellum igitur tē ....(superāre, 1st person

singular, future).

....

III. PRACTICE SENTENCES. (Before translating each, read the Latin aloud twice.)

a. Magister noster mē laudat et tē laudābit. ....

....

b. Līberī virī perīcula nostra superābunt. ....

....

c. Fīliī nostrī puellās pulchrās amant. ....

....

d. Culpās multās habēmus et semper habēbimus. ....

....

e. Pulchra patria nostra est lībera. ....

....

f. Līberī virī estis; patriam pulchram habēbitis. ....

....

g. Magistrī līberī officiō cūram dabunt. ....

....

h. Sī īram tuam superābis, tē superābis. ....

....

i. Propter nostrōs animōs multī sunt līberī. ....

....

j. Habetne animus tuus satis sapientiae? ....

....

CHAPTER VI

SUM: Future and Imperfect Indicative;
POSSUM: Present, Future, and Imperfect Indicative;
Complementary Infinitive.

OBJECTIVES:

1. To learn the active indicative future and imperfect of ESSE.

2. To learn the active indicative present, future and imperfect of POSSE.

3. To know the syntax governing complementary infinitives.

I. GRAMMAR.
    (MEMORIZE PARADIGMS (MODELS) AND VOCABULARY BY REPEATING THEM ALOUD!)

    1. In order to say "TO BE ABLE," the Romans originally combined the
        root POT (POTIS, able) with ESSE to produce POTESSE which later
        became .... = TO BE ABLE, CAN.

    2. POSSE, like DĒBĒRE, is regularly followed by an infinitive whose
        function is to .... the meaning of POSSE.

    3. A complementary infinitive (Circle one.)

            has its own subject   uses that of DĒBĒRE or POSSE

    4. Conjugate ESSE in the active indicative tenses indicated:

		Present		Future		Imperfect	
		Latin	English	Latin	English	Latin	English
	1.	....	....	....	....	....	....
Singular	2.	....	....	....	....	....	....
	3.	....	....	....	....	....	....
	1.	....	....	....	....	....	....
Plural	2.	....	....	....	....	....	....
	3.	....	....	....	....	....	....

5. Conjugate POSSE in the active tenses indicated:

		Present		Future		Imperfect	
		Latin	English	Latin	English	Latin	English
Singular	1.	....	....	....	....	....	....
Singular	2.	....	....	....	....	....	....
Singular	3.	....	....	....	....	....	....
Plural	1.	....	....	....	....	....	....
Plural	2.	....	....	....	....	....	....
Plural	3.	....	....	....	....	....	....

CHAPTER VI

NAME _____ SECTION _____ DATE _____

II. DRILL.

A. Translate the following into English or Latin.

a. erat .... f. We shall be able to ....

b. poterit .... g. I can ....

c. poterāmus .... h. you were able to ....

d. erō .... i. he will be ....

e. poterunt .... j. we were ....

B. Supply the correct forms of the words shown in parentheses and translate:

a. Librī Graecōrum ....(esse; imperfect) vērī.

....

b. Liber vester ....(esse; future) vērus.

....

c. Librī nostrī ....(esse; present) vērī.

....

d. Nōn ....(posse; 1st person plural; imperfect)

tolerāre vitia tyrannōrum. ....

....

e. Nōn ....(posse, 1st person plural, future) tolerāre librōs

malōs. ....

f. Nōn ....(posse, 1st person plural, present) tolerāre

vestrās culpās. ....

g. Ubi ....(posse, 2nd person singular, imperfect)

superāre tyrannōs? Ibi. ....

....

h. Ubi ....(posse, 2nd person singular, present) superāre

Insidiās tyrannōrum? Ibi. ....

....

i. Ubi ....(posse, 2nd person singular, future) superāre

Insidiās nostrās? Ibi. ....

....

j. Insidiae Graecōrum ....(esse, imperfect) perpetuae.

....

III. PRACTICE SENTENCES. (Before translating each, read the Latin aloud twice.)

a. Patria vestra erat lībera. ....

b. Amīcus vester erit tyrannus. ....

c. Ubi tyrannus est, virī nōn possunt esse līberī. ....

....

d. Tyrannī multa vitia semper habēbunt. ....

....

e. Tyrannum nostrum superāre dēbēmus. ....

f. Poteritis perīcula tyrannī vidēre. ....

....

g. Insidiās tyrannī nōn tolerābis. ....

h. Dēbēs virōs līberōs dē tyrannīs monēre. ....

....

i. Librī bonī vērīque poterant patriam cōnservāre. ....

....

j. Tyrannī sapientiam bonōrum librōrum superāre nōn poterunt. ....

....

....

CHAPTER VII

Third Declension: Nouns

OBJECTIVE:

To learn the declension of the third declension consonant-stem nouns in the masculine, feminine and neuter genders.

I. GRAMMAR.
(MEMORIZE PARADIGMS (MODELS) AND VOCABULARY BY REPEATING THEM ALOUD!)

1. Gender presents a great difficulty in the 3rd declension because the latter includes a variety of all genders. The safest proceudre is to memorize the gender. One of the declension's features, however, is that nouns denoting human beings are ..../ or .... according to meaning.

2. In the 3rd declension, the gender of nouns (can, cannot) ordinarily be identified by the endings as was the case with 1st and 2nd declension nouns.

3. Give the information requested below for each of the third declension endings listed.

	Case(s)	Number	Gender(s)
1. -um	....	....	....
2. -ibus	....	....	....
3. -a	....	....	....
4. -ēs	....	....	....
5. -is	....	....	....
6. -em	....	....	....
7. -e	....	....	....
8. -ī	....	....	....

4. Give the proper nominative singular form of the adjective MAGNUS, A, UM to accompany the following 3rd declension nouns:

   a. tempus .... f. pāx ....

   b. virtūs .... g. rēx ....

   c. labor .... h. corpus ....

   d. cīvitās .... i. virgō ....

   e. mōs .... j. amor ....

CHAPTER VII

NAME _____ SECTION _____ DATE _____

II. DRILL.

A. Translate the following into English or Latin.

    a. labōrēs multī   ....

    b. pācis perpetuae   ....

    c. cīvitātum parvārum   ....

    d. cīvitāte parvā   ....

    e. tempora mala   ....

    f. great virtues (dir. obj.) ....

    g. with great courage   ....

    h. our times (subj.)   ....

    i. to/for our times   ....

    j. by my love   ....

B. Supply the correct forms of the words shown in parentheses and translate.

    a. Audēbimus servāre ....(pāx).

    ....

    b. ....(mōrēs) ....(homō, genitive plural)

    sunt malī. ....

    c. Propter ....(virtūs), audēbimus ibi remanēre.

    ....

    d. In ....(labor) est ....(virtūs).

    ....

    e. Nōn habēbitis satis ....(tempus).

    ....

    f. Sine ....(litterae), nōn possumus servāre ....

    (amor). ....

g. Graecae ....(virgō) erant bellae.

....

h. Nōn habēmus ....(pāx) in ....(cīvitās, plural).

....

i. Mōs .... (labor, genitive) semper dabit ....(mōrēs)

............(homō, plural). ....

....

j. Poterisne superāre sine ....(virtūs).

....

II. PRACTICE SENTENCES. (Before translating each, read the Latin aloud twice.)

a. Pecūnia est nihil sine mōribus bonīs. ....

....

b. Mōrēs hominis bonī erunt bonī. ....

....

c. Hominī litterās dabunt. ....

d. Magnum amōrem pecūniae in multīs hominibus vidēmus. ....

....

e. Cīvitās nostra pācem hominibus multīs dabit. ....

....

f. Sine bonā pāce cīvitātēs temporum nostrōrum nōn valēbunt. ..

....

g. In multīs cīvitātibus terrīsque pāx nōn poterat valēre. ....

....

h. Virgō pulchra amīcōs mōrum bonōrum amat. ....

....

i. Hominēs magnae virtūtis tyrannōs superāre audēbunt. ....

....

j. Amor patriae in cīvitāte nostrā valet. ....

....

CHAPTER VIII

Third Conjugation (DŪCŌ):
Present Infinitive, Present and Future Indicative,
Present Imperative Active.

OBJECTIVE:

To learn the conjugation of the active infinitive present, the indicative present and future and the imperative present of the Latin third conjugation verbs.

I. GRAMMAR.
    (MEMORIZE PARADIGMS (MODELS) AND VOCABULARY BY REPEATING THEM ALOUD!)

1. What vowels mark the endings of the active indicative present in the third conjugation?

    ....

2. What vowels mark the endings of the active indicative future in the third conjugation?

    ....

3. Give the active imperative present for the verbs dūcere, dīcere, facere, ferre, mittere and pōnere:

2nd Sing.	....	....	....
2nd Plur.	....	....	....
2nd Sing.	....	....	....
2nd Plur.	....	....	....

4. Give information requested for each of the following endings:

	Tense	Number	Person
a. -imus	....	....	....
b. -ēs	....	....	....
c. -unt	....	....	....
d. -et	....	....	....
e. -itis	....	....	....

	Tense	Number	Person
f. -ēmus	....	....	....
g. -ō	....	....	....
h. -ent	....	....	....
i. -it	....	....	....
j. -ētis	....	....	....
k. -is	....	....	....
l. -am	....	....	....

CHAPTER VIII

NAME _____ SECTION _____ DATE _____

II. DRILL.

A. Given the verbs MITTERE, to send, AGERE, to do, SCRĪBERE, to write, PŌNERE, to put, translate the following into English or Latin.

a. mittent ....   m. they are putting ....

b. mittunt ....   n. we shall put ....

c. mitte ....   o. put (imp. sing.) ....

d. mittimus ....   p. he puts ....

e. mittētis ....   q. they will put ....

f. agit ....   r. I shall put ....

g. agam ....   s. you (sing.) are putting ....

h. agēmus ....   t. you (plu.) will put ....

i. agis ....   u. put (imp. plu.) ....

j. scrībet ....   v. we put ....

k. scrībite ....   w. you (plu.) are putting ....

l. scrībitis ....   x. he will put ....

B. Supply the correct forms of the words shown in parentheses and translate.

a. Ratiō ....(agere; present) hominēs.

....

b. ....(scrībere; 2nd person singular, imperative) nihil

dē cōpiīs. ....

c. Post bellum, ...(mittere; 1st person singular, future)

litterās. ....

d. ....(mittere; 3rd person singular, present) cōpiam

librōrum. ....

e. Grātiās ....(agere; 2nd person plural, future) amīcō
vestrō. ....

C. Translate the following:

a. Dare to tolerate good judgement.

....

b. He will lead the troops to (toward) glory.

....

c. The state will thank the tyrant.

....

d. Your (sing) friend is sending a letter.

....

e. Because of your work, you will have an abundance of money.

....

III. PRACTICE SENTENCES. (Before translating each, read the Latin aloud twice.)

a. Hominem ad mē dūcunt. ....

b. Dūc hominem ad mē, et hominī grātiās agam. ....

....

c. Dum tyrannus cōpiās dūcit, possumus nihil agere. ....

....

d. Librōs dē pāce scrībēmus. ....

e. Puerī magistrō grātiās nōn agunt. ....

....

f. Paucī cīvitātī nostrae grātiās agent. ....

g. Tyrannus magnās cōpiās ex cīvitāte nostrā dūcet. ....

....

h. Magna cōpia pecūniae hominēs ad sapientiam nōn dūcit. ....

....

i. Dūcimusne saepe hominēs ad ratiōnem? ....

....

j. Ratiō hominēs ad bonam vītam dūcere potest. ....

....

CHAPTER IX

Demonstrative Pronouns: HIC, ILLE, ISTE

OBJECTIVES:

1. To learn the declension and use of the Latin demonstratives HIC, ILLE and ISTE.

2. To observe carefully the peculiar forms of the genitive and dative singular.

3. To note that demonstratives can be used as adjectives or pronouns.

4. To learn the peculiar declension of certain first and second declension adjectives which have -IUS in the genitive singular and -Ī in the dative singular.

I. GRAMMAR.
    (MEMORIZE PARADIGMS AND VOCABULARY BY REPEATING THEM ALOUD!)

1. Adjectives/pronouns used by the Romans to .... persons

    or things are called ....

2. The declension difficulties of the Latin demonstratives come chiefly

    from the irregularity of three singular cases. They are:

    ....

3. For all practical purposes, Latin demonstratives are declined like

    adjectives of the .... declension and therefore like

    paradigm ....

4. Give the information requested below for each of the Latin adjectives/
    pronouns listed.

	Case(s)	Number	Gender(s)	Translation(s)
a. istud	....	....	....	....
b. istī	....	....	....	....
c. istīs	....	....	....	....
d. istīus	....	....	....	....

	Case(s)	Number	Gender(s)	Translation(s)
e. istō	....	....	....	....
f. illārum	....	....	....	....
g. illī	....	....	....	....
h. ille	....	....	....	....
i. illa	....	....	....	....
j. illum	....	....	....	....
k. haec	....	....	....	....
1. huius	....	....	....	....
m. hoc	....	....	....	....
n. huic	....	....	....	....
o. hunc	....	....	....	....
p. hōrum	....	....	....	....
q. iste	....	....	....	....
r. hōs	....	....	....	....
s. illam	....	....	....	....
t. illae	....	....	....	....

6. Give the information requested below for each of the following Latin
   irregular adjectives of the first and second declensions.

	Case(s)	Number	Gender(s)	Translation(s)
a. ūllīus	....	....	....	....
b. nūllīus	....	....	....	....
c. nūllam	....	....	....	....
d. ūllō	....	....	....	....
e. tōtō	....	....	....	....
f. tōtīus	....	....	....	....
g. tōtī	....	....	....	....
h. sōlō	....	....	....	....

	Case(s)	Number	Gender(s)	Translation(s)
i. sōlī	....	....	....	....
j. sōlum	....	....	....	....
k. ūnīus	....	....	....	....
l. ūnum	....	....	....	....
m. ūnī	....	....	....	....
n. alterīus	....	....	....	....
o. aliī	....	....	....	....
p. aliā	....	....	....	....
q. aliud	....	....	....	....
r. alterī	....	....	....	....
s. aliōrum	....	....	....	....
t. alterum	....	....	....	....

CHAPTER IX

NAME _____ SECTION _____ DATE _____

II. DRILL.

    A. Translate the following into English or Latin.

        a. haec puella ....

        b. illa puella ....

        c. huic temporī ....

        d. huius temporis ....

        e. illī puerō ....

        f. nūllī librō ....

        g. huic cīvitātī sōlī ....

        h. tōtīus patriae ....

        i. nūllīus ratiōnis ....

        j. huius cīvitātis sōlīus ....

        k. no reason (acc.) ....

        l. to/for the whole country ....

        m. to/for one city ....

        n. no books (acc.) ....

        o. by another book ....

        p. to/for that boy alone ....

        q. those times (acc.) ....

        r. that time (nom.) ....

        s. of that girl alone ....

        t. to/for one girl ....

    B. Supply the correct form of the words shown in parentheses and translate.

        a. ....(tōtus, -a, -um) locus erat vērus.

        ....

b. Habētis .... (nūllus, -a, -um) vitia.

....

c. Vidēbimus ....(sōlus, -a, -um) bona loca.

....

d. Fāma ....(iste, -a, -ud) locī remanet.

....

e. Multī locī ....(hic, haec, hoc) librī errant.

....

C. Translate the following:

a. No passage of this letter is true.

....

b. Another friend will thank my son.

....

c. Lead your troops into that region.

....

d. Without any reason, they will call.

....

e. Your eyes will see those places.

....

III. PRACTICE SENTENCES. (Before translating each, read the Latin <u>aloud</u> twice.)

a. Hī tōtam cīvitātem dūcent (dūcunt). ....

....

b. In illō librō illa dē hōc homine scrībet (scrībam). ....

....

c. Ūnus vir istās cōpiās in hanc terram dūcit (dūcet). ....

....

d. Hunc librum dē aliō bellō scrībimus (scrībēmus). ....

....

e. Tōta patria huic sōlī grātiās agit (aget). ....

....

f. Hic vir sōlus mē dē vitiīs huius tyrannī monēre poterat. ....

....

g. Nūllās cōpiās in alterā terrā habētis. ....

....

h. Illī sōlī nūlla perīcula in hōc consiliō vident. ....

....

i. Nōn sōlum mōrēs sed etiam īnsidiās illīus laudāre audēs. ....

....

j. Propter īnsidiās enim ūnīus hominis haec cīvitās nōn valet. .....

....

CHAPTER X

Fourth Conjugation and -IŌ Verbs of the Third:
Present and Future Indicative, Present Imperative,
and Infinitive Active.

OBJECTIVE:

To learn the active infinitive present, the active indicative present
and future, and the active imperative present of Latin verbs of the
fourth conjugation (AUDIŌ, AUDĪRE) and -IŌ verbs of the third conjugation (CAPIŌ, CAPERE).

I. GRAMMAR.
    (MEMORIZE PARADIGMS AND VOCABULARY BY REPEATING THEM ALOUD!)

    1. Give the information requested for the following infinitives:

		Conjugation	Meaning
a.	vīvere	....	....
b.	invenīre	....	....
c.	valēre	....	....
d.	vocāre	....	....
e.	vidēre	....	....
f.	fugere	....	....
g.	venīre	....	....
h.	facere	....	....
i.	servāre	....	....
j.	capere	....	....
k.	errāre	....	....
l.	scrībere	....	....
m.	docēre	....	....
n.	audīre	....	....
o.	dūcere	....	....
p.	agere	....	....
q.	audēre	....	....

	Conjugation	Meaning
r. tolerāre	....	....
s. remanēre	....	....
t. habēre	....	....

2. Complete the conjugation of the following and give the English meaning of each person:

		vīvō	fugiō	veniō ... .
Singular	1.			
	2.	....	....	....
	3.	....	....	....
Plural	1.	....	....	....
	2.	....	....	....
	3.	....	....	....

3. Complete the conjugation of the following and give the Latin meaning for each person:

		I shall act	I shall make	I shall find ......
Singular	1.			
	2.	....	....	....
	3.	....	....	....
Plural	1.	....	....	....
	2.	....	....	....
	3.	....	....	....

4. Give the Latin imperative for the following:

(sing)	Write	Live	Hear ....
(plur)	Write	Live	Hear ....

CHAPTER X

NAME _____ SECTION _____ DATE _____

II. DRILL.

   A. Translate the following into English or Latin.

       a. scrībe ....   k. I shall lead ....

       b. fugimus ....   l. She will get ....

       c. inveniētis ....   m. We shall hear ....

       d. vīvent ....   n. You will do (plu.) ....

       e. facis ....   o. I am making ....

       f. venīmus ....   p. It is coming ....

       g. agitis ....   q. We live ....

       h. capiunt ....   r. You are fleeing (plu.) ....

       i. audīte ....   s. Find (imper. sing.) ....

       j. dūc ....   t. Write (imper. plur.) ....

   B. Supply the correct form of the words shown in parentheses and
       translate:

       a. Tempus ....(fugere, present).

       ....

       b. ....(vīvere; 1st person plural; future) semper in

       pāce. ....

       c. Sapientia senectūtis ....(invenīre, future) pācem.

       ....

       d. Nātūra .... (invenīre; future) viam.

       ....

       e. Cum fīliā nostrā, ...(fugere, 3rd person plural,

       present) ad viam. ....

C. Translate the following:

    a. Love will find you.

    ....

    b. The hour is fleeing.

    ....

    c. They come to see you often.

    ....

    d. Our daughter finds peace in nature.

    ....

    e. You will make a good road.

    ....

III. PRACTICE SENTENCES. (Before translating each, read the Latin <u>aloud</u> twice.)

    a. Cum fīliā tuā fuge. ....

    b. Tempus fugit; hōrae fugiunt; senectūs venit. ....

    ....

    c. In patriam vestram veniunt. ....

    d. Fīliam tuam in illā cīvitāte inveniēs. ....

    ....

    e. Tyrannus viam in hanc cīvitātem invenit. ....

    ....

    f. Ad tē cum magnīs cōpiīs venīmus. ....

    ....

    g. Iste bellum semper facit. ....

    ....

    h. Multī hominēs illa faciunt sed haec nōn faciunt. ....

    ....

    i. Magnam cōpiam librōrum faciam. ....

    ....

j. In librīs virōrum antīquōrum multam philosophiam et sapientiam

inveniētis. ....

....

CHAPTER XI

Personal Pronouns EGO and TŪ; Demonstrative Pronouns IS and ĪDEM.

OBJECTIVES:

1. To learn to decline and to use the first and second person personal pronouns in the singular and the plural.

2. To learn to decline and to use the colorless or relatively weak Latin demonstrative IS, EA, ID which serves as the third person personal pronoun, and its derivative ĪDEM, EADEM, IDEM.

I. GRAMMAR.
    (MEMORIZE PARADIGMS AND VOCABULARY BY REPEATING THEM ALOUD!)

    1. How many genders does the declension of the Latin first and second personal pronouns include? (Circle one.)

        one   two   three

    2. How many genders does the declension of the Latin third person personal pronouns include? (Circle one.)

        one   two   three

    3. The nominatives of the Latin personal pronouns were: (Circle one.)

        (a) not used by the Romans except for stress

        (b) never expressed because they were dictated by the verb ending

    4. The pronouns NOSTRUM and VESTRUM were used by the Romans as (Circle one.)

        possessive genitives   partitive genitives   objective genitives

    5. The pronouns NOSTRĪ and VESTRĪ were used by the Romans as (Circle one.)

        possessive genitives   partitive genitives   objective genitives

6. Decline below the first and second personal pronouns in the singular and plural and give the translations.

	1st PERSON		2nd PERSON	
	Latin	English Meaning	Latin	English Meaning

Singular

Nom	....	....	....	....
Gen	....	....	....	....
Dat	....	....	....	....
Acc	....	....	....	....
Abl	....	....	....	....

Plural

Nom	....	....	....	....
Gen	....	....	....	....
Dat	....	....	....	....
Acc	....	....	....	....
Abl	....	....	....	....

7. Decline below the third personal (demonstrative) pronoun in the singular and plural and give the translations.

	Masculine		Feminine		Neuter	
	Latin	English Meaning	Latin	English Meaning	Latin	English Meaning

Singular

Nom	....	....	....	....	....	....
Gen	....	....	....	....	....	....
Dat	....	....	....	....	....	....
Acc	....	....	....	....	....	....
Abl	....	....	....	....	....	....

	Masculine		Feminine		Neuter	
	Latin	English Meaning	Latin	English Meaning	Latin	English Meaning
			Plural			
Nom	....	....	....	....	....	....
Gen	....	....	....	....	....	....
Dat	....	....	....	....	....	....
Acc	....	....	....	....	....	....
Abl	....	....	....	....	....	....

8. Decline below in the singular and plural the derivative of the third person Latin personal pronoun which means THE SAME.

	Masculine		Feminine		Neuter	
	Latin	English Meaning	Latin	English Meaning	Latin	English Meaning
			Singular			
Nom	....	....	....	....	....	....
Gen	....	....	....	....	....	....
Dat	....	....	....	....	....	....
Acc	....	....	....	....	....	....
Abl	....	....	....	....	....	....
			Plural			
Nom	....	....	....	....	....	....
Gen	....	....	....	....	....	....
Dat	....	....	....	....	....	....
Acc	....	....	....	....	....	....
Abl	....	....	....	....	....	....

CHAPTER XI

NAME _____ SECTION _____ DATE _____

II. DRILL.

    A. Translate the following in English or Latin.

        a. nōbīs (abl)............   k. it ....

        b. īdem ....   l. of us (partitive) ....

        c. vestrī ....   m. I ....

        d. vōs ....   n. you (sing. dir. obj.) ....

        e. mihi ....   o. for you (plu.) ....

        f. eius (fem) ....   p. by her ....

        g. eō (neuter) ....   q. his ....

        h. nostrum ....   r. for me ....

        i. eam ....   s. the same man ....

        j. eī (masc) ....   t. its ....

    B. Supply the correct form of the word shown in parentheses and translate:

        a. .... (nēmō) cōpiās mittet.

        ....

        b. Dā ....(ego) tempus.

        ....

        c. Fīlia ....(is) bene sentit.

        ....

        d. Multī ....(vōs, genitive) nunc venient.

        ....

        e. Mittō nēminem ad ....(ea, feminine).

        ....

    C. Translate the following:

        a. The same girl will send their books.

        ....

b. Her dear daughter flees with a friend.

....

c. No one of us must write.

....

d. Give him one hour.

....

e. You will not find it without care.

....

III. PRACTICE SENTENCES. (Before translating each, read the Latin <u>aloud</u> twice.)

a. Hī tibi id dabunt. ....

b. Ego vōbīs id dabō. ....

c. Vōs eīs id dabitis. ....

d. Eī idem dabō. ....

e. Nōs eī ea dabimus. ....

f. Ille mihi id dabit. ....

g. Vōbīs librōs eius dabimus. ....

h. Nōbīs librōs eōrum dabis. ....

i. Pecūniam eōrum tibi dabimus. ....

j. Pecūniam eius mihi dabunt. ....

k. Librōs eius ad eam mittēmus. ....

l. Librum eius ad tē mittam. ....

m. Ille autem pecūniam eōrum ad nōs mittet. ....

....

n. Eās cum eā mittimus. ....

o. Eum cum eīs mittō. ....

p. Eōs cum amīcīs eius mittēmus. ....

....

q. Tū mē cum amīcō eōrum mittēs. ....

....

r. Vōs mēcum ad amīcum eius mittunt. ....

....

s. Nōs tēcum in terram eōrum mittit. ....

....

t. Tē cum eō ad mē mittent. ....

....

CHAPTER XII

Perfect Active System of All Verbs; Principal Parts.

OBJECTIVES:

1. To learn the four forms which constitute the principal parts of Latin verbs and to memorize the principal parts of the Latin verbs learned thus far.

2. To learn to conjugate the active indicative perfect, pluperfect and future perfect i.e. the active perfect system for Latin verbs of all four conjugations.

I. GRAMMAR.
(MEMORIZE PARADIGMS AND VOCABULARY BY REPEATING THEM ALOUD!)

1. The names of the forms which constitute the principal parts of Latin

   verbs listed in the sequence used in vocabularies and dictionaries are:

   ....

2. Give the principal parts for the four Latin conjugations using the pattern verbs we have used in our text with the English meaning under each one:

1st ....

....

2nd ....

....

3rd ....

....

3rd (IŌ verbs)...... ....

....

4th ....

....

3. Up to this chapter, you have learned the first two principal parts
    of 27 Latin verbs in addition to five pattern verbs. Nine were from
    the first conjugation, seven from the 2nd, six from the 3rd, two
    from 3rd (IŌ verbs) and three from the 4th. Add to these the first
    two principal parts of the irregular verbs SUM and POSSUM.

    Give the three remaining principal parts for each verb listed.

    a. cōgitō ....

    b. dō   ....

    c. habeō   ....

    d. videō   ....

    e. agō   ....

    f. scrībō ....

    g. faciō   ....

    h. fugiō   ....

    i. sentiō ....

    j. veniō   ....

4. Give the principal parts of the following:

    Sum   ....

    Possum   ....

5. The stem of all the active perfect tenses is that of the ....

    tense; i.e. the ....principal part.

6. The .... tense of Esse is used as the endings of the

    active indicative ....tense; and the ....

    tense of ESSE (except for the 3rd person plural) is used as the

    endings of the active indicative .... tense in all

    conjugations.

7. Using the verbs indicated conjugate the tenses below:

Active Indicative

		Perfect (Remanēre)		Pluperfect (Vīvere)		Future Perfect (Vincere)	
		Latin	English	Latin	English	Latin	English
Singular	1.	....	....	....	....	....	....
Singular	2.	....	....	....	....	....	....
Singular	3.	....	....	....	....	....	....
Plural	1.	....	....	....	....	....	....
Plural	2.	....	....	....	....	....	....
Plural	3.	....	....	....	....	....	....

CHAPTER XII

NAME _____ SECTION _____ DATE _____

II. DRILL.

A. Translate the following into English or Latin.

a. Dīxeram .... f. They fled ....

b. Mīserimus .... g. We shall have taught ....

c. Vēnistī .... h. She had had ....

d. Vīcerant .... i. You saw (plur) ....

e. Vocāvērunt .... j. I had thought ....

B. Supply the correct form of the words in parentheses and translate.

a. ....(remanēre; 3rd person singular, perfect) diū in

Asiā. ....

b. Dī ad caelum eām ....(mittere, future perfect).

....

c. Caesar rēgī lībertātem ....(dare, pluperfect).

....

d. Dē nātūrā litterās ....(scrībere; 1st person plural,

perfect). ....

e. Fīlium tuum diū ....(vidēre; 2nd person singular,

pluperfect). ....

C. Translate the following.

a. They conquered nature.

....

b. You had said (plural) nothing.

....

c. We shall have conquered old age.

....

d. He felt much courage.

....

e. By treachery he had preserved his nation.

....

III. PRACTICE SENTENCES. (Before translating each, read the Latin <u>aloud</u> twice.)

a. Hī remānsērunt (remanent; remanēbunt; remānserant). ....

....

b. Rēgēs Asiam vīcērunt (vincent; vincunt; vīcerant). ....

....

c. Caesar in eandem terram vēnerat (vēnit; venit; veniet). ....

....

d. Caesar eadem dīxit (dīcit; dīxerat; dīcet). ....

....

e. Vōs nōbīs pācem dedistis (dabitis; dederātis). ....

....

f. Diū vīxerat (vīxit; vīvet). ....

....

g. Id bene fēcerās (faciēs; fēcistī; facis). ....

....

h. Eum in eōdem locō invēnērunt (invēnerant; invenient). ....

....

i. Deus hominibus lībertātem dederat (dedit; dat; dabit). ....

....

j. Vōs fuistis (erātis; estis; eritis; fuerātis) virī līberī. ....

....

....

CHAPTER XIII

Reflexive Pronouns and Possessives;
Intensive Pronoun.

OBJECTIVES:

1. To learn the declension and the use of the Latin reflexive pronouns.

2. To learn the use of the third person reflexive possessive adjectives
    SUUS, -A, -UM.

3. To learn the declension and the use of the Latin intensive pronoun/
    adjective IPSE, -A, -UM.

I. GRAMMAR.
    (MEMORIZE PARADIGMS AND VOCABULARY BY REPEATING THEM ALOUD!)

    1. Reflexive pronouns are "bent back" to reflect on the (Circle one.)

            object   verb   subject

    2. Since reflexive pronouns are used only in the predicate and reflect
        one of the above, they have no need for which of the following cases?

            genitive   accusative   nominative

    3. Give all the meanings of the following (include those learned in
        Chapter XI):

        a. mihi ....

        b. vōbīs ....

        c. nōs ....

        d. meī ....

        e. sē ....

        f. vōs ....

        g. tē ....

        h. suī ....

        i. vestrī ....

        j. tibi ....

        k. nōbīs ....

1. nostrī ....

m. tuī ....

n. mē ....

o. sibi ....

4. Decline the Latin intensive pronoun.

	Masculine		Feminine		Neuter	
	Latin	English Meaning	Latin	English Meaning	Latin	English Meaning
Singular
Nom	....	....	....	....	....	....
Gen	....	....	....	....	....	....
Dat	....	....	....	....	....	....
Acc	....	....	....	....	....	....
Abl	....	....	....	....	....	....
Plural
Nom	....	....	....	....	....	....
Gen	....	....	....	....	....	....
Dat	....	....	....	....	....	....
Acc	....	....	....	....	....	....
Abl	....	....	....	....	....	....

5. For the first and second persons, the Romans indicated possession by
.... (my), ...(your; singular), ...
(our) and ....(your; plural), whether the possessive adjective
was used as a reflexive or not.

6. For the third person, the Romans normally indicated possession by

    ....(his, her, its, their) when the possessive adjec-

    tive was used in the predicate and referred to the subject. Other-

    wise, they regularly indicated possession by the genitives

    ...., ... and ....

    (literally of him, of her, of it, of them).

CHAPTER XIII

NAME _____ SECTION _____ DATE _____

II. DRILL.

A. Supply the correct form of the words in parentheses and translate.

a. Scrīpsit nōmen ....(possession; masculine; refers

to subj.). ....

b. Dīxit nōmen ....(possession; feminine; does not refer

to subj.). ....

c. Magister numquam .... (reflexive) docuit sapientiam.

....

d. Magister numquam .... (regular personal feminine)

docuit sapientiam. ....

e. Ante bellum, cōpiae cum amīcīs ....(his) sē iūnxērunt.

....

B. Translate the following:

a. They gave themselves courage.

....

b. They gave them courage.

....

c. I said it to myself.

....

d. They said it to me.

....

e. He will preserve his (someone else's) freedom.

....

III.   PRACTICE SENTENCES.   (Before translating each, read the Latin <u>aloud</u> twice.)

    a.   Cicero came to Caesar himself ....

    b.   Cicero esteemed himself and you esteem yourself. ....

....

    c.   Caesar eum servāvit. ....

    d.   Caesar sē servāvit. ....

    e.   Rōmānī sē servāvērunt. ....

    f.   Rōmānī eōs servāvērunt. ....

    g.   Rōmānī eum servāvērunt. ....

    h.   Caesar amīcum suum servāvit. ....

    i.   Caesar amīcum eius servāvit. ....

    j.   Nōs nōn servāvērunt. ....

    k.   Nōs servāvimus. ....

    l.   Mihi nihil dedit. ....

    m.   Mihi nihil dedī. ....

    n.   Sibi nihil dedit. ....

    o.   Sibi nihil dedērunt. ....

    p.   Mē vīcī. ....

    q.   Mē vīcērunt. ....

CHAPTER XIV

I-stem Nouns of the Third Declension;
Ablative of Means, Accompaniment and Manner.

OBJECTIVES:

1. To complete our study of the third declension of Latin nouns with the
   I-stem nouns.

2. To learn to recognize and understand the precise meaning of the Latin
   ablatives of means or instrument, of accompaniment, and of manner.

I. GRAMMAR.
   (MEMORIZE PARADIGMS AND VOCABULARY BY REPEATING THEM ALOUD!)

   1. The third declension nouns we studied in Chapter VII are known
      as (Circle one.)

           I-stems   Consonant stems   a-stems

   2. The first group or category of third declension I-stem nouns are

      called **parisyllabic** because the nominative and genitive have the

      same number of syllables. The nominative ending of nouns in this

      group is either .... or ....

   3. The majority of nouns in the **parisyllabic** group are (Circle one.)

           masculine   feminine

   4. The second group or category of I-stem nouns has a stem ending in

      two consonants. The nominative ending of nouns in this group is

      either .... or ....

   5. The third group or category of I-stem nouns contains only a few

      neuter nouns whose nominatives end either in ....,

      ...., or ....

   6. The i in the third declension I-stem nouns appears in nouns of all
      three genders in only one case, the (Circle one.)

           ablative singular   genitive plural   accusative plural

7. The only other consistent appearance of the i in third declension
    I-stem nouns is in the ablative singular and the nominative and
    accusative plural of which of the three groups? (Circle one.)

        First (m. + f.)   Second (m. + f.)   Third (n)

8. Give the declensions of the second declension noun VIR and the
    irregular third declension I-stem noun VIS.

	Latin	English	Latin	English
		Singular		
Nom	....	....	....	....
Gen	....	....	....	....
Dat	....	....	....	....
Acc	....	....	....	....
Abl	....	....	....	....
		Plural		
Nom	....	....	....	....
Gen	....	....	....	....
Dat	....	....	....	....
Acc	....	....	....	....
Abl	....	....	....	....

9. The Latin ablative of means/instrument answers the question (Circle
    one.)

        with whom?   with what?   how?

10. The Latin ablative of manner answers the question (Circle one.)

        with whom?   with what?   how?

11. The Latin ablative of accompaniment answers the question (Circle one.)

        with whom?   with what?   how?

12. With the Latin ablative of accompaniment the English preposition
    WITH is rendered in Latin by (Circle one.)

        no preposition   CUM

13. With the Latin ablative of instrument the English preposition WITH
    is rendered in Latin by (Circle one.)

        no preposition   CUM

14. Give the information requested for the following:

		Translation	Type of Ablative
a.	with a citizen	....	....
b.	by death	....	....
c.	with feeling	....	....
d.	with skill	....	....
e.	by sea	....	....
f.	iūre	....	....
g.	cum virīs	....	....
h.	oculīs meīs	....	....
i.	cum cūrā	....	....
j.	labōre meō	....	....

CHAPTER XIV

NAME _____ SECTION _____ DATE _____

II. DRILL.

  A. Translate the following into English or Latin.

  a. arte ....   k. by force ....

  b. marī ....   l. of strength ....

  c. partis ....   m. of citizens ....

  d. animālia ....   n. with the citizens ....

  e. artium ....   o. with strength ....

  f. mare ....   p. seas (nominative) ....

  g. urbēs ....   q. a sea (accusative) ....

  h. partium ....   r. by a citizen ....

  i. animālī ....   s. for the city ....

  j. nūbēs ....   t. by the sea ....

  B. Supply the correct form of the words in parentheses and translate.

  a. Cīvēs .... (urbs; genitive plural) bella gerunt.

  ....

  b. ....(mare; accusative) tenuit.

  ....

  c. Cum ....(virtūs) mortem tolerāvērunt.

  ....

  d. Cum ....(ars) urbem tenuerātis.

  ....

  e. Rēx trāns .... (urbs) cucurrit.

  ....

C. Translate the following:

a. He managed the city with his own strength.

    ....

b. The force of the seas restrained them.

    ....

c. They wrote part of the opinions.

    ....

d. We dragged the tyrant across the city.

    ....

e. Death will never possess the soul.

    ....

III. PRACTICE SENTENCES. (Before translating each, read the Latin <u>aloud</u> twice.)

a. Ipsī lībertātem cīvium suōrum servāverant. ....

    ....

b. Pars cīvium per urbem ad mare cucurrit. ....

    ....

c. Great is the strength of the arts. ....

d. Ipse cīvitātem vī cōpiārum tenuit. ....

    ....

e. Illa animālia multōs hominēs in mare trāxērunt. ....

    ....

f. Eum ad mortem trāns terram eius trāxistis. ....

    ....

g. Vīs illōrum marium erat magna. ....

    ....

h. Sententiās magnās pulchrāsque ex virīs antīquīs trāximus. ....

    ....

i. The citizen did that with money (with care; with his own friends).

....

j. Multa bella cum Rōmānīs gessit. ....

....

k. Cīvitātem magnā cum sapientiā gessērunt. ....

....

l. Hoc magnā cum arte dīxistī. ....

....

m. Cum cūrā trāns urbem cucurrimus. ....

....

n. Magnā cum parte cīvium ad nōs vēnit. ....

....

o. Iūra cīvium vī vincet. ....

....

CHAPTER XV

Imperfect Indicative Active of the Four Conjugations;
Ablative of Time.

OBJECTIVES:

1. To complete our study of the active voice of the indicative of all
    conjugations of Latin verbs by learning the conjugation of the
    imperfect tense.

2. To understand the use of the imperfect tense of the indicative by
    comparing it and its English meaning with the perfect tense and its
    English meaning.

3. To continue our study of the precise meaning and use of the Latin
    ablative with or without prepositions by learning the ablative of time.

I. GRAMMAR.
    (MEMORIZE PARADIGMS AND VOCABULARY BY REPEATING THEM ALOUD!)

    1. The three elements which are used to construct the indicative

        imperfect tense in all Latin conjugations are the ....

        stem, the .... sign and the active ....

        endings.

    2. In the fourth conjugation, the .... sign is altered by the

        addition of the letter .... preceding it taken from the

        .... conjugation.

    3. The Latin perfect tense indicates a .... act in the

        past which can, using a camera metaphor, be compared to a ....

        Therefore, the English translations of DŪXĪ would be ....

        or .... or ....

    4. The Latin imperfect tense indicates a .... or

        .... or .... action in the past which

        can, using a camera metaphor, be compared to a ....

        Therefore, English translations of DŪCĒBAM would be ....

        or .... or ....

5. In Latin expressions denoting time when or within which something occurred, the English prepositions AT, ON, IN or WITHIN are (Circle one.)

  translated not translated

6. To note the similarities and differences between them, conjugate the active indicative future and imperfect of the following verbs as indicated below.

		Future			Imperfect		
		stem	sign ending	English Meaning	stem	sign ending	English Meaning

TIMĒRE

	1.	......	....	....	....	......	....	....	....
Singular	2.	......	....	....	....	......	....	....	....
	3.	......	....	....	....	......	....	....	....
	1.	......	....	....	....	......	....	....	....
Plural	2.	......	....	....	....	......	....	....	....
	3.	......	....	....	....	......	....	....	....

MITTERE

	1.	......	....	....	....	......	....	....	....
Singular	2.	......	....	....	....	......	....	....	....
	3.	......	....	....	....	......	....	....	....
	1.	......	....	....	....	......	....	....	....
Plural	2.	......	....	....	....	......	....	....	....
	3.	......	....	....	....	......	....	....	....

7. Give the indicated information for the following:

		Translation	Type of Ablative
a.	with the girls	....	....
b.	with a letter	....	....
c.	with great courage	....	....
d.	with courage	....	....
e.	in one hour	....	....
f.	at the same time	....	....
g.	within a few hours	....	....
h.	at that time	....	....
i.	by means of supplies	....	....
j.	with money	....	....

CHAPTER XV

NAME _____ SECTION _____ DATE _____

II. DRILL.

A. Translate the following.

a. We were daring.

....

k. They kept coming.

....

b. She threw.

....

l. They were fearing.

....

c. He has taken.

....

m. We used to dare.

....

d. I habitually wrote.

....

n. You (sing) fled.

....

e. We used to understand.

....

o. She was throwing.

....

f. They came.

....

p. He used to take.

....

g. I kept hearing.

....

q. I heard.

....

h. You (plur) have changed.

....

r. I wrote.

....

i. They have feared.

....

s. We understood.

....

j. You (sing) were fleeing.

....

t. You (plur) used to change.

....

B. Supply the correct form of the words in parentheses and translate.

a. Itaque pater fīliam suam .... (exspectāre, imperfect).

....

b. Inter cīvēs, multī sententiās suās ....(mutāre,

future). ....

c. ....(intellegere, 2nd person plural, perfect) iura?

....

d. Italiam patribus ....(committere, 3rd person plural,

imperfect). ....

e. Nautae mare numquam ....(timēre, future).

....

C. Translate the following.

a. They drove the tyrant out.

....

b. You used to entrust part of the city to the troops.

....

c. Your father understood their opinion.

....

d. We were throwing his letter into the sea.

....

e. By philosophy, he used to change their character.

....

III. PRACTICE SENTENCES. (Before translating each, read the Latin aloud twice.)

a. Iste tyrannus sē semper laudābat. ....

....

b. In urbem cum amīcō meō veniēbam. ....

....

c. Bella magna cum virtūte gerēbātis. ....

....

d. Itaque Rōmānī Graecōs vīcērunt. ....

....

e. Vīdistīne patrem meum eō tempore? ....

....

f. Ubi hanc pecūniam invēnistis? ....

g. Vēnērunt, et idem nōbīs dīcēbat. ....

....

h. Librōs eius numquam intellegēbam. ....

....

i. Vītam nostram numquam mutāvimus. ....

j. Rōmānī mōrēs temporum antīquōrum laudābant. ....

....

CHAPTER XVI

Adjectives of the Third Declension

OBJECTIVE:

To learn the declension of Latin adjectives of the third declension.

I. GRAMMAR.
    (MEMORIZE PARADIGMS AND VOCABULARY BY REPEATING THEM ALOUD!)

1. Adjectives of the third declension are declined, except in the
    ablative singular of the masculine and feminine, like which of the
    following third declension noun groups? (Circle one.)

                consonant-stem   I-stem

2. The majority of Latin third declension adjectives belong to the
    group having how many nominative singular endings? (Circle one.)

                one   two   three

3. The ablative singular ending for all third declension adjectives is

    the same as that for the neuter third declension I-stem nouns ending

    in -E, -AL, or -AR. The ending is, therefore, ...

4. Masculine and feminine third declension adjectives follow the

    pattern of the I-stem noun .... and the

    neuter ones of the I-stem noun ....

5. The two cases in which the characteristic I appears in all genders

    of the third declension adjectives are the ....

    singular and the .... plural.

6. Decline the Latin adjectives which correspond to the following:

POWERFUL

Masculine	Feminine Singular	Neuter
Nom	....	....
Gen	....	....
Dat	....	....
Acc	....	....
Abl	....	....

Plural

Nom	....	....
Gen	....	....
Dat	....	....
Acc	....	....
Abl	....	....

ALL, EVERY

Masculine	Feminine Singular	Neuter
Nom	....	....
Gen	....	....
Dat	....	....
Acc	....	....
Abl	....	....

Plural

Nom	....	....
Gen	....	....
Dat	....	....
Acc	....	....
Abl	....	....

SWIFT

Masculine	Feminine	Neuter

Singular

	Masculine	Feminine	Neuter
Nom	....	....	....
Gen	....	....	....
Dat	....	....	....
Acc	....	....	....
Abl	....	....	....

Plural

	Masculine	Feminine	Neuter
Nom	....	....	....
Gen	....	....	....
Dat	....	....	....
Acc	....	....	....
Abl	....	....	....

7. Can third declension adjectives be used with nouns of the first and

    second declension?   ....

CHAPTER XVI

NAME _____ SECTION _____ DATE _____

II. DRILL.

    A. Translate the following:

        a. omnī marī

        ....

        b. omnium partium

        ....

        c. omnia nōmina

        ....

        d. dulcī matrī

        ....

        e. omnī bonā arte

        ....

        f. beātae mātrī

        ....

        g. omnium bellōrum

        ....

        h. beātō hominī

        ....

        i. omnia maria

        ....

        j. dulcī puellā

        ....

        k. dulcī mātre

        ....

        l. omnia bella

        ....

        m. beātō homine

        ....

        n. omnī bonae artī

        ....

        o. dulcī puellae

        ....

        p. vī celerī

        ....

        q. omnī parte

        ....

        r. omnis bonae artis

        ....

        s. omnium rēgum

        ....

        t. beātā mātre

        ....

    B. Supply the correct form of the words in parentheses and translate.

        a. .... (dulcis, e) memoriae senectūtem iuvant.

        ....

b. Mātrēs aetatem ....(brevis, e) semper timēbunt.

....

c. Quam ....(celer, celeris, celere) aetātēs sunt.

....

d. Pater amīcōs ....(miser) filiōrum ....

(acer) iūvit. ....

e. Corpore ....(fortis, e) saepe vincebāmus.

....

C. Translate the following:

a. All laws are not good laws.

....

b. We retained memories of a difficult life.

....

c. In a short period of time the war had changed.

....

d. Within an hour you expected every friend.

....

e. They drew strength from the pleasant woman's courage.

....

III. PRACTICE SENTENCES. (Before translating each, read the Latin aloud twice.)

a. Aetās longa saepe est difficilis. ....

....

b. Aetās difficilis potest esse beāta. ....

....

c. Quam brevis erat dulcis vīta eius! ....

....

d. Memoria dulcis aetātis omnēs hominēs adiuvat. ....

....

e. In omnī terrā multōs virōs fortēs vidēbitis. ....

....

f. Illud bellum breve erat difficile. ....

....

g. Omnia perīcula paucīs hōrīs superāvimus. ....

....

h. Brevī tempore omnia iūra cīvium mūtābit. ....

....

i. Difficilem artem lībertātis dulcis nōn intellēxērunt. ....

....

j. Hominēs officia difficilia in omnibus terrīs timent. ....

....

CHAPTER XVII

The Relative Pronoun.

OBJECTIVE:

To learn the declension and the use of Latin relative pronouns.

I. GRAMMAR.
    (MEMORIZE PARADIGMS AND VOCABULARY BY REPEATING THEM ALOUD!)

1. A relative pronoun in English or in Latin is so called because it

    .... or .... to a noun or another pronoun

    called its ....

2. Relative clauses are parts of sentences which are termed   (Circle one.)

    simple   complex

3. A relative pronoun usually begins a clause termed   (Circle one.)

    principal   coordinate   subordinate

4. The term ANTECEDENT comes from ANTE + CĒDERE which means ....

    ....

5. The case of the relative pronoun is determined by its (Circle one.)

    function in its clause   antecedent

6. The gender and number of the relative pronoun are determined by its
    (Circle one.)

    function in its clause   antecedent

7. Decline the Latin relative pronouns:

	Masculine		Feminine		Neuter	
	Latin	English Meaning	Latin	English Meaning	Latin	English Meaning
Singular						
Nom	....	....	....	....	....	....
Gen	....	....	....	....	....	....
Dat	....	....	....	....	....	....
Acc	....	....	....	....	....	....
Abl	....	....	....	....	....	....
Plural						
Nom	....	....	....	....	....	....
Gen	....	....	....	....	....	....
Dat	....	....	....	....	....	....
Acc	....	....	....	....	....	....
Abl	....	....	....	....	....	....

CHAPTER XVII

NAME _____ SECTION _____ DATE _____

II. DRILL.

A. Translate the following into English or Latin.

a. Puer cuius liber

....

b. Oculōs quōs

....

c. Vīrēs quibus

....

d. Litterās quae

....

e. Id quod

....

f. Eam quācum (see W.p.52 n.9.)

....

g. Cīvēs quī

....

h. Iūs quō

....

i. Urbs per quam

....

j. Locum quem

....

k. The state (subj.) which (dir. obj.) ....

l. The daughter (dir. obj.) whose

....

m. The seas (dir. obj.) across which

....

n. The books (subj.) in which

....

o. The woman (subj.) to whom

....

p. The citizen (dir. obj.) who

....

q. The friends (dir. obj.) with whom

....

r. The letter (subj.) which (subj.)

....

s. The sons (subj.) whom

....

t. The girls (dir. obj.) who

....

B. Supply the correct form of the words in parentheses and translate.

a. Vēritās ....(quī, quae, quod) dīxistī erat difficilis.

....

b. Factum ....(quī, quae, quod, ablative) vīcimus erat

magnum. ....

c. Vīderam fēminam ....(quī, quae, quod, genitive) fīlius

fūgerat. ....

d. Sentīmus amīcitiam ....(quī, quae, quod) sē nōn

mūtābit. ....

e. Viae trāns ....(quī, quae, quod) currēbant erant longae.

....

C. Translate the following:

a. The treachery which we feared is evil.

....

b. You will lead those troops with whom you came.

....

c. He will destroy the friendship which we have.

....

d. They neglected the man whose deeds were great.

....

e. The age which is beginning will be happy.

....

III. PRACTICE SENTENCES. (Before translating each, read the Latin aloud twice.)

a. Cīvēs laudāvērunt quōs mīserātis. ....

....

b. Cīvem laudāvērunt quī patriam servāverat. ....

....

c. Cīvem laudāvērunt cuius fīlius patriam servāverat. ....

....

d. Cīvēs laudāvērunt quōrum fīliī patriam servāverant. ....

....

e. Cīvem laudāvērunt cui patriam commīserant. ....

....

f. Cīvēs laudāvērunt quibus patriam commīserant. ....

....

g. Tyrannus urbēs dēlēvit ex quibus cīvēs fūgerant. ....

....

h. Tyrannus urbēs dēlēvit in quās cīvēs fūgerant. ....

....

i. Puellīs quās laudābat librōs dedit. ....

....

j. Virō cuius fīliam amās vītam suam commīsit. ....

....

CHAPTER XVIII

Present, Imperfect and Future Indicative Passive
of LAUDŌ and MONEŌ;
Ablative of Agent.

OBJECTIVES:

1. To learn the forms of the PASSIVE VOICE of the present, imperfect, and future indicative and the present infinitive of the Latin first and second conjugations.

2. To understand the use of the passive voice.

3. To learn the function of the ablative of personal agent and its relationship with the ablative of means/instrument and the passive voice.

I. GRAMMAR.
   (MEMORIZE PARADIGMS AND VOCABULARY BY REPEATING THEM ALOUD!)

   1. When a verb is in the active voice, the action is performed by the (Circle one.)

              subject   object

   2. When a verb is in the passive voice, the action is performed by the (Circle one.)

              subject   object

   3. When a verb is in the active voice, the action is received by the (Circle one.)

              subject   object

   4. When a verb is in the passive voice, the action is received by the (Circle one.)

              subject   object

   5. In the following sentences, underline the performer of the action:

      a. The player struck his opponent.

      b. The opponent was struck by the player.

6. In the following sentences, underline the receiver of the action:

   a. The player struck his opponent.

   b. The opponent was struck by the player.

7. The passive infinitive present forms of LAUDŌ and MONEŌ are

   .... and .... The English meanings

   of those infinitives are .... and ....

8. Five of the six passive personal endings are characterized by the

   consonant letter ....

9. Using the first conjugation verb IŪVĀRE, conjugate the following
   tenses of the indicative in the passive voice:

		Present		Future		Imperfect	
		Latin	English	Latin	English	Latin	English
	1.	....	....	....	....	....	....
Singular	2.	....	....	....	....	....	....
	3.	....	....	....	....	....	....
	1.	....	....	....	....	....	....
Plural	2.	....	....	....	....	....	....
	3.	....	....	....	....	....	....

10. Using the second conjugation verb DĒLĒRE, conjugate the following
    tenses of the indicative in the passive voice:

		Present		Future		Imperfect	
		Latin	English	Latin	English	Latin	English
	1.	....	....	....	....	....	....
Singular	2.	....	....	....	....	....	....
	3.	....	....	....	....	....	....

		Present		Future		Imperfect	
		Latin	English	Latin	English	Latin	English
	1.	....	....	....	....	....	....
Plural	2.	....	....	....	....	....	....
	3.	....	....	....	....	....	....

11. Provide the information indicated for the following ablatives:

		Preposition (if none, so indicate)	Used for people, things, etc.
a.	means/instrument	....	....
b.	accompaniment	....	....
c.	manner	....	....
d.	time	....	....
e.	personal agent	....	....

CHAPTER XVIII

NAME_____ SECTION _____ DATE _____

II. DRILL.

A. Translate the following into English or Latin.

a. Vocābiminī

k. She used to be feared.

....

b. Vocābāminī

l. She is being feared.

....

c. Vocāminī

m. She will be feared.

....

d. Docēbantur

n. I shall be expected.

....

e. Docentur

o. I am expected.

....

f. Docēbuntur

p. I was being expected.

....

g. Mutābimur

q. We habitually were seen.

....

h. Mutābāmur

r. We shall be seen.

....

i. Tenēbāris

s. It is tolerated.

....

j. Tenēberis

t. It will be tolerated.

....

B. Supply the correct passive form of the words in parentheses and translate:

a. In lūdō puellae ....(docēre, present).

....

b. Puerī ā magistrō nōn ....(movēre, future).

....

c. Omnēs urbēs ā cōpiīs ....(dēlēre, imperfect).

....

d. Mora cōnsiliōrum ā nōbīs ....(expectāre, imperfect).

....

e. Hīs generibus insidiārum ....(servāre, 1st person

plural, future). ....

C. Translate the following:

a. The school will be changed by this plan.

....

b. We were not being helped by that type of game.

....

c. He is not being affected even by his own father.

....

d. You will not be feared by your citizens.

....

e. The letter used to be held by my daughter.

....

III. PRACTICE SENTENCES. (Before translating each, read the Latin <u>aloud</u> twice.)

a. Mē terrent; ab eīs terreor; vī eōrum terreor. ....

....

b. Ab amīcīs movēbātur; cōnsiliīs eōrum movēbātur. ....

....

c. Vīribus hominum nōn dēlēmur, sed possumus īnsidiīs dēlērī. ....

....

d. Tū ipse nōn mūtāris, sed nōmen tuum mūtātur. ....

....

e. Librī huius generis puerīs a magistrō dabantur sed paucī legēbantur.

....

f. Lībertās populō ab rēge brevī tempore dabitur. ....

....

g. Patria nostra ā cīvibus fortibus etiam nunc servārī potest. ....

....

h. Fortūnā aliōrum monērī dēbēmus. ....

....

i. Ab amīcīs potentibus adiuvābimur. ....

....

j. Omnēs virōs nostrōs laudāmus, quī virtūte et vēritāte moventur, nōn

amōre suī. ....

....

CHAPTER XIX

Perfect Passive System of all Verbs;
Interrogative Pronouns and Adjectives.

OBJECTIVES:

1. To learn to conjugate the passive indicative perfect, pluperfect and future perfect, i.e., the passive perfect system for Latin verbs of all four conjugations.

2. To learn to decline and to use the Latin interrogative pronouns and adjectives.

I. GRAMMAR.
   (MEMORIZE PARADIGMS AND VOCABULARY BY REPEATING THEM ALOUD!)

   1. The Latin perfect passive indicative is composed of the passive

      .... and the .... tense of ESSE.

   2. The Latin pluperfect passive indicative is composed of the passive

      .... and the .... tense

      of ESSE.

   3. The Latin passive indicative future perfect is composed of the passive

      .... and the .... tense

      of ESSE.

   4. Conjugate the following tenses in the passive voice using the Latin verb AMĀRE.

	Present			Perfect		
	Latin	Eng. 1	Eng. 2	Latin	Eng. 1	Eng. 2
1.	....	....	....	....	....	....
Singular 2.	....	....	....	....	....	....
3.	....	....	....	....	....	....

		Present			Perfect		
		Latin	Eng. 1	Eng. 2	Latin	Eng. 1	Eng. 2
	1.	....	....	....	....	....	....
Plural	2.	....	....	....	....	....	....
	3.	....	....	....	....	....	....

5. Conjugate the following tenses in the passive voice using the Latin verb TERRERE.

		Imperfect		Pluperfect	
		Latin	English	Latin	English
	1.	....	....	....	....
Singular	2.	....	....	....	....
	3.	....	....	....	....
	1.	....	....	....	....
Plural	2.	....	....	....	....
	3.	....	....	....	....

6. Conjugate the following tenses in the passive voice using the latin verb MITTERE.

		Future (Chapter XXI)		Future Perfect	
		Latin	English	Latin	English
	1.	....	....	....	....
Singular	2.	....	....	....	....
	3.	....	....	....	....
	1.	....	....	....	....
Plural	2.	....	....	....	....
	3.	....	....	....	....

7. The declension of the Latin interrogative pronouns in the singular is almost the same as that of the .... pronouns.

8. The singular cases of the two above types of pronouns which differ
   are the ...., the ...., the
   .... and the ....

9. The declension of the singular of the .... adjectives
   and the .... pronouns is exactly the same.

10. The declension of the plural of the .... pronouns,
    the .... adjectives and the ....
    pronouns is exactly the same.

11. The distinctions between the following are best remembered by filling
    in the chart as indicated.

	Modifies noun (yes or no)	Expressed or implied antecedent (has or has not)	Introduces a direct question (yes or no)	Sentence ends with question mark (yes or no)
interr. pronoun	....	....	....	....
interr. adj.	....	....	....	....
relative pronoun	....	....	....	....

12. Fill in the following declensions.

Interr. Pronoun
Singular

	M Latin	M English	F Latin	F English	N Latin	N English
Nom	....	....	....	....	....	....
Gen	....	....	....	....	....	....
Dat	....	....	....	....	....	....
Acc	....	....	....	....	....	....
Abl	....	....	....	....	....	....

Interr. Adjective (& Relative Pronoun)
Singular

	M Latin	M English	F Latin	F English	N Latin	N English
Nom	....	....	....	....	....	....
Gen	....	....	....	....	....	....
Dat	....	....	....	....	....	....
Acc	....	....	....	....	....	....
Abl	....	....	....	....	....	....

13. Fill in the following declension.

Interr. Pronoun & Adjective (& Relative Pronoun)
Plural

	M Latin	M English	F Latin	F English	N Latin	N English
Nom	....	....	....	....	....	....
Gen	....	....	....	....	....	....
Dat	....	....	....	....	....	....
Acc	....	....	....	....	....	....
Abl	....	....	....	....	....	....

CHAPTER XIX

NAME_____ SECTION _____ DATE_____

II. DRILL

    A. Translate the following into English or Latin.

        1. Verbs

            a. dūcō (three meanings) ....

            b. dūcor (two meanings) ....

            c. dūxī (three meanings) ....

            d. ductus, -a, -um sum (two meanings) ....

            e. dūcēbam (three meanings) ....

            f. dūcēbar (three meanings) ....

            g. dūxeram (one meaning) ....

            h. dūcam (one meaning)..

            i. dūxerō (one meaning) ....

            j. ductus, -a, -um erō (one meaning) ....

            k. We were taken or have been taken ....

            l. We were taking ....

            m. We shall take ....

            n. We shall have taken ....

            o. We shall have been taken ....

        2. Interrogative pronouns/adjectives and Relative pronouns: (give all meanings).

            a. Quārum? ....

            b. Quis? ....

            c. Quōrum ....

            d. Quid? ....

            e. Quod ....

            f. Quam ....

g. Quem? ....

h. Quā ....

i. Quō? ....

j. Whose (sing.) ....

k. Who? (m. nom. sing.) ....

l. What? (n. acc. sing.) ....

m. Whom? (f. sing.) ....

n. Whom (m. sing.) ....

o. Which (acc. sing.) ....

B. Supply the correct form of the words in parentheses and translate:

a. Ūnā hōrā iūdicium ....(dare, passive pluperfect).

....

b. Ā ....(quis? plural) ....(ēicere, 2nd person

plural, passive perfect)? ....

c. Brevī tempore ....(dēlēre, 1st person plural, passive

future perfect). ....

d. ....(quis? genitive plural) iūdicium ....

(parāre, passive perfect)? ....

e. Ā ....(quis? singular) .... (līberāre, 3rd

person plural, passive pluperfect)? ....

C. Translate the following:

a. The old man had been neglected.

....

b. By what new game had they been helped?

....

c. At what time will she have been saved?

....

d. We had been neglected by him for a long time.

....

e. By what name were you called then?

....

III. PRACTICE SENTENCES. (Before translating each, read the Latin aloud twice.)

a. Magister ā quō liber parātus est labōre superātur. ....

....

b. Puerum quī servātus est ego ipse vīdī. ....

....

c. Senem cuius fīliī servātī sunt numquam vīdī. ....

....

d. Ā cīve quī missus erat pāx et lībertās laudātae sunt............

....

e. Ā cīvibus quī missī erant amīcitia laudāta est. ....

....

f. Cuī liber datus est (dabātur), datus erat? ....

....

g. Quid puerō dictum est cuī liber datus est? ....

....

h. Quis servātus est? Quī puer servātus est? ....

....

i. Cuius fīliī servātī sunt? ....

j. Quis missus est? ....

k. Quōs in urbe vīdistī? ....

l. Quae ā tē ibi inventa sunt? ....

....

m. Ā quibus hoc dictum est? ....

....

n. Quōrum fīliī ab eō laudātī sunt? ....

....

o. Quod perīculum vōs terret? ....

....

CHAPTER XX

Fourth Declension;
Ablatives of "Place from Which" and "Separation."

OBJECTIVES:

1. To learn to decline Latin nouns of the fourth declension.

2. To understand the use of the Latin ablatives used to express "place from which" and "separation."

I. GRAMMAR.
   (MEMORIZE PARADIGMS AND VOCABULARY BY REPEATING THEM ALOUD.)

1. The letter which characterizes all but two endings of the fourth declension nouns is ....

2. The two cases whose endings do not begin with the characteristic letter are the .... and the ....

3. The gender of most fourth declension Latin nouns is ....

4. The only feminine noun of the fourth declension which occurs with any frequency is .... It is declined like nouns of the .... gender.

5. Neuter nouns of the fourth declension declined like CORNŪ are (Circle one.)

    frequent   average   rare

6. The ablative of "place from which" emphasizes the idea of .... and requires one of the three prepositions ...., ..., or ....

7. The ablative of "separation" from things or people after verbs meaning to free, to lack or to deprive would be placed under which of the following columns of our ablative chart?

    No Preposition   Optional Preposition   Always Preposition

8. The ablative of separation from things with most other verbs would be placed under which of the following?

       No Preposition   Optional Preposition   Always Preposition

9. The ablative of separation from people would be placed under which of the following?

       No Preposition   Optional Preposition   Always Preposition

10. Complete the following declension (be sure to include the long vowel signs -).

	Latin	English	Latin	English

Singular

	Latin	English	Latin	English
Nom	Metus	....	Cornū	....
Gen	....	....	....	....
Dat	....	....	....	....
Acc	....	....	....	....
Abl	....	....	....	....

Plural

Nom	....	....	....	....
Gen	....	....	....	....
Dat	....	....	....	....
Acc	....	....	....	....
Abl	....	....	....	....

CHAPTER XX

NAME _____ SECTION _____ DATE _____

II. DRILL.

  A. Translate the following into English or Latin.

      a. senatuī ....   k. of the senate ....

      b. versū .... l. for the band ....

      c. metuum .... m. the enjoyment (subj.) ....

      d. manūs (subject) .... n. with verses ....

      e. senatum .... o. the horns (dir. obj.) ....

      f. metibus .... p. of the dread ....

      g. versūs (dir. obj.) .... q. with the hands ....

      h. manuī .... r. the profits (subj.) ....

      i. metū .... s. by the senate ....

      j. manus .... t. the anxiety (subj.) ....

  B. Supply the correct form of the words in parentheses and translate:

      a. In Graeciā ....(metus) servitūtis superāvimus.

      ....

      b. Neque .... (frūctus, plural) neque ....
      (metus, plural) caruistī. ....

      c. Hae .... (manus, plural) ....(servitūs,
      singular) liberātae erant. ....
      ....

      d. In .... (manus) amīci ....(metus) carent.
      ....

      e. Iūdicium ā rēge contrā ....(senātus) datum est.
      ....

C. Translate the following:

    a. The fear of crime has terrified the people.

....

    b. In Greece, the profits of slavery were understood.

....

    c. Important verses had been written by my son.

....

    d. Laws against crime save the citizens.

....

    e. He lacks the common friendship of the people.

....

III. PRACTICE SENTENCES. (Before translating each, read the Latin <u>aloud</u> twice.)

    a. Quis ad nōs eō tempore vēnit? ....

....

    b. Quid ab eō dictum est? ....

    c. Eōs sceleribus istīus tyrannī līberāvimus. ....

....

    d. Nunc omnī metū carent. ....

    e. Fīliī eōrum bonōs librōs in lūdīs nostrīs cum studiō legunt. ....

....

    f. Hī versūs nōbīs grātiās magnās agunt. ....

....

    g. Nam illī miserī nunc frūctūs pācis lībertātisque sine metū habent. ..

....

....

    h. Virī bonī cōpiā hōrum frūctuum numquam carēbunt. ....

....

CHAPTER XXI

Third and Fourth Conjugations:
Passive Voice of Indicative and Present Infinitive.

OBJECTIVE:

To learn the passive voice of the indicative and the present infinitive
of the third and fourth conjugation verbs.

I. GRAMMAR.
   (MEMORIZE PARADIGMS AND VOCABULARY BY REPEATING THEM ALOUD!)

1. Give the present infinitives of the following verbs in the voice
   indicated: parō, moveō, mittō, ēiciō, inveniō.

   to prepare   to move   to send   to drive out   to find

ACTIVE

   ....

   to be   to be   to be   to be   to be
   prepared   moved   sent   driven out   found

PASSIVE

   ....

2. Conjugate in Latin the entire tense, voice, and mood indicated for
   each verb.

		I send	I am sent	I drive out	I am driven out	I find	I am found
	1.	......	....	....	....	......	......
Singular	2.	......	....	....	....	......	......
	3.	......	....	....	....	......	......
	1.	......	....	....	....	......	......
Plural	2.	......	....	....	....	......	......
	3.	......	....	....	....	......	......

3. Conjugate in Latin the entire tense, voice, and mood indicated for
    each verb.

I shall send   **I shall be sent**

	1.	....	....
Singular	2.	....	....
	3.	....	....
	1.	....	....
Plural	2.	....	....
	3.	....	....

I shall drive out   **I shall be driven out**

	1.	....	....
Singular	2.	....	....
	3.	....	....
	1.	....	....
Plural	2.	....	....
	3.	....	....

I shall find   **I shall be found**

	1.	....	....
Singular	2.	....	....
	3.	....	....
	1.	....	....
Plural	2.	....	....
	3.	....	....

4. Conjugate in Latin the entire tense, voice, and mood indicated for each verb.

I used to send   **I used to be sent**

		I used to send	I used to be sent
Singular	1.	....	....
	2.	....	....
	3.	....	....
Plural	1.	....	....
	2.	....	....
	3.	....	....

		I used to drive out	I used to be driven out
Singular	1.	....	....
	2.	....	....
	3.	....	....
Plural	1.	....	....
	2.	....	....
	3.	....	....

		I used to find	I used to be found
Singular	1.	....	....
	2.	....	....
	3.	....	....
Plural	1.	....	....
	2.	....	....
	3.	....	....

CHAPTER XXI

NAME _____ SECTION _____ DATE _____

II. DRILL.

A. Translate the following into English or Latin.

a. Vincēminī

....

k. He was commanding

....

b. Scitur

....

l. They were seized

....

c. Iubēbimur

....

m. You will be compared (sing.)

....

d. Rapiēbantur

....

n. I am ordering

....

e. Continēbar

....

o. To be seized

....

f. Sciēris

....

p. They will be restrained

....

g. Rapiar

....

q. We were being carried away

....

h. Continēbor

....

r. It will be known

....

i. Scīminī

....

s. I conquer

....

j. Sciēminī

....

t. I am conquered

....

B. Supply the correct form of the words in parentheses and translate.

a. Causa .... (scīre; passive, present).

....

b. In fīnibus .... (continēre; passive, 1st person plural, future). ....

c. Laudis causā versūs .... (scrībere; passive, 3rd person plural, imperfect). ....

d. Gentēs mundī ā mē ....(iubēre; passive, present). ....

e. Virtūte vestrā .... (scīre; passive, 2nd person plural, future). ....

C. Translate the following:

a. It will be ordered for the sake of the people.

....

b. The territory was being seized.

....

c. We used to write a letter often.

....

d. The boundaries are well known.

....

e. The people will never be restrained.

....

III. PRACTICE SENTENCES. (Before translating each, read the Latin <u>aloud</u> twice.)

a. Quis mittitur (mittētur, mittēbātur, missus est)? ....

....

b. Ā quō hae litterae mittentur (missae sunt, mittuntur)? ....

....

c. Quid dictum est (dīcēbātur, dīcētur, dīcitur)? ....

....

d. Diū neglegēris/neglegēminī (neglēctus es/neglēctī estis). ....

....

e. Cīvitātis causā eum rapī iussērunt. ....

....

f. Animus eius pecūniā tangī nōn poterat. ....

....

g. Amor patriae in omnī animō sentiēbātur (sentiētur, sentītur, sēnsus

est). ....

....

h. Amōre patriae cum aliīs cīvibus iungimur (iungēbāmur, iungēmur). ....

....

....

i. Sapientia et vēritās in stultīs hominibus nōn invenientur (inveniuntur,

inventae sunt). ....

....

j. Sapientia etiam multā pecūniā nōn parātur (parābitur, parāta est). ..

....

....

CHAPTER XXII

Fifth Declension;
Summary of Ablatives.

OBJECTIVES:

1. To learn to decline Latin nouns of the fifth declension.

2. To review the ablative ideas and expressions which have been studied so far.

I. GRAMMAR.
(MEMORIZE PARADIGMS AND VOCABULARY BY REPEATING THEM ALOUD!)

  1. The letter which characterizes all endings of the fifth declension

     nouns is ....

  2. The gender of fifth declension Latin nouns is ....

  3. The only exception to the above is ....

     whose gender is regularly ....

  4. Complete the declension of the following:

	Singular		Plural	
	Latin	English	Latin	English
Nom	fidēs	....	....	....
Gen	....	....	....	....
Dat	....	....	....	....
Acc	....	....	....	....
Abl	....	....	....	....

5. Reconstruct the following chart of Latin ablatives, indicating
    what Latin prepositions, if any, are used.

	Type	NEVER Prep.	Optional	ALWAYS Prep.
1.	....	....	....	....
2.	....	....	....	....
3.	....	....	....	....
4.	....	....	....	....
5.	....	....	....	....
6.	....	....	....	....
7.	....	....	....	....
8.	....	....	....	....

CHAPTER XXII

NAME _____ SECTION _____ DATE _____

II. DRILL.

    A. Translate the following into English or Latin.

        a. Rērum   k. to the republic (ind. obj.)

        ....

        b. Diēbus   l. with hope

        ....

        c. Speī (dative)   m. on that day

        ....

        d. Fidem   n. for the faith

        ....

        e. Spēs (nom. sing.)   o. in many days

        ....

        f. Rē pūblicā   p. business (dir. obj.)

        ....

        g. Diē   q. uncertain hope (subj.)

        ....

        h. Spēs (acc. plur.)   r. new things (dir. obj.)

        ....

        i. Fideī (genitive)   s. within one day

         ....

        j. Diēs (nom. plur.)   t. of hopes

        ....

    B. Complete the following:

                                       Type of
                         Translation   Ablative

        a. In urbe remānsit.   ....

	Translation	Type of Ablative
b. Ūnā hōrā veniet.	....	....
c. Eō tempore vēnit.	....	....
d. Cum eīs vēnit.	....	....
e. Ex urbe vēnit.	....	....
f. Igne carent.	....	....
g. Illud igne factum est.	....	....
h. Id ab eīs factum est.	....	....
i. Id cum fidē factum est.	....	....

C. Supply the correct form of the words in parentheses and translate.

a. .... (fidēs) gentium fortis est.

....

b. ....(spēs) pācis numquam tollētur.

....

c. Ignis animī ....(fidēs; means) alitur.

....

d. Multī cīvēs ....(rēs pūblica; genitive) eripiuntur.

....

e. Numerus ....(diēs; genitive, plural) incertus est.

....

III. PRACTICE SENTENCES. (Before translating each, read the Latin aloud twice.)

a. Rem pūblicam magnā cum cūrā gessit. ....

....

b. Eō diē multās rēs cum spē parāvērunt. ....

....

c. Paucīs diēbus Cicerō rem pūblicam ē perīculō ēripiet. ....

....

d. Omnēs rēs pūblicās metū liberāvistī. ....

....

e. Terra hominēs frūctibus bonīs alit. ....

....

CHAPTER XXIII

Participles.

OBJECTIVES:

1. To learn to identify and to decline the Latin active and passive present, perfect and future verbal adjectives called participles.

2. To learn the uses and translations of the Latin participles.

I. GRAMMAR.
   (MEMORIZE PARADIGMS AND VOCABULARY BY REPEATING THEM ALOUD!)

   1. Latin verbs which follow the four regular conjugations and are transitive (i.e. take a direct object) have how many verbal adjectives called participles? (Circle one.)

      one   two   three   four   five   six

   2. Of the Latin participles, how many are active and what are they?

      ....

   3. Of the Latin participles, how many are passive and what are they?

      ....

   4. The present stem is used to construct which Latin participles?

      VOICE   TENSE   ENDING

   5. The participial (fourth principal part) stem is used to construct which Latin participles?

      VOICE   TENSE   ENDING

6. Using the verbs indicated, fill in the following chart showing the
    participles of all conjugations.

MŪTĀRE

	Active		Passive	
	Latin	English	Latin	English
Present	....	....	....	....
Perfect	....	....	....	....
Future	....	....	....	....

DOCĒRE

	Active		Passive	
	Latin	English	Latin	English
Present	....	....	....	....
Perfect	....	....	....	....
Future	....	....	....	....

LEGERE

	Active		Passive	
	Latin	English	Latin	English
Present	....	....	....	....
Perfect	....	....	....	....
Future	....	....	....	....

RAPERE

	Active		Passive	
	Latin	English	Latin	English
Present	....	....	....	....
Perfect	....	....	....	....
Future	....	....	....	....

SENTĪRE

	Active		Passive	
	Latin	English	Latin	English
Present	....	....	....	....
Perfect	....	....	....	....
Future	....	....	....	....

7. The Latin active future participle conveys the idea that the accomplishment of an action is **imminent** and is translated by .... or ....

8. The Latin passive future participle conveys the idea that an action is necessary, highly desirable, or strongly indicated and is translated by .... or ....

9. The active present participle is declined like the adjective .... and the others like the adjective ....

10. The tense of a Latin participle is relative to that of the .... verb and is not .... The key is to ask yourself if the action of the participle is .... with, ... to or .... to the action of the main verb.

11. Latin participles can often be more effectively translated by (Circle one.)

specific English participle expressions	clauses or phrases fitting context

CHAPTER XXIII

NAME _____ SECTION _____ DATE_____

II. DRILL

   A. Translate the following into English or Latin in accordance with their tense and voice.

     a. pressūrus   k. having been seen

     ....

     b. premēns   l. about to write

     ....

     c. cupītūrī   m. writing

     ....

     d. datūrōs   n. fit to be seen

     ....

     e. premendus   o. due to be written

     ....

     f. cupīta   p. fit to be sent

     ....

     g. dandum   q. seeing

     ....

     h. cupiendī   r. having been written

     ....

     i. pressus   s. going to send

     ....

     j. cupientēs   t. about to see

     ....

   B. Supply the correct form of the words in parentheses and translate.

     a. Orātor .... (invenīre; perfect participle) dīcere nōn

     potest. ....

b. Signum .... (dare; present participle) cucurrit.

....

c. Nōs, urbem .... (opprimere; future active participle),

....

cōnsilium ōrātōris audīvimus. ....

d. Dōna .... (cupere; perfect participle) rapuit.

....

e. Signa .... (vidēre, present participle), rēx intelleget.

....

C. Translate the following:

a. The gifts, having been displayed, were sent.

....

b. Shall we ever be happy desiring pleasant things only?

....

c. The senate, about to change the law, feared the people.

....

d. The city, having to be overwhelmed, was subdued by fire.

....

e. Seeking pleasant things, we have neglected faith.

....

III. PRACTICE SENTENCES. (Before translating each, read the Latin aloud twice.)

a. Captus nihil dīxit. ....

b. Dōna dantibus grātiās ēgit. ....

c. Aliquem dōna petentem nōn amō. ....

....

d. Ad lūdum tuum fīlium meum docendum mīsī. ....

....

e. Hīs īnsidiīs territī vītam miseram vīvēmus. ....

....

f. Illī virī miserī, ā tyrannō vīsī, trāns fīnem cucurrērunt. ....

....

g. Aliquem nōs timentem timēmus. ....

h. Senex, ab amīcīs monitus, ad nōs fūgit. ....

....

i. Quis hīs perīculīs līberātus deīs grātiās nōn dabit? ....

....

j. Fidem habentibus nihil est incertum. ....

....

CHAPTER XXIV

Ablative Absolute;
Passive Periphrastic; Dative of Agent.

OBJECTIVE:

To learn the use of participles, or verbal adjectives, studied in the previous lesson in two idiomatic and very common Latin constructions:

a. The Ablative Absolute, a relatively independent phrase usually set off by commas.

b. The Passive Periphrastic (with Dative of Agent, not Ablative of Personal Agent).

I. GRAMMAR.
(MEMORIZE PARADIGMS AND VOCABULARY BY REPEATING THEM ALOUD!)

1. A noun or a pronoun modified by a verbal adjective called a

.................., with both those parts in the ....

case, constitutes an idiomatic and very common construction in Latin

called the ....

2. The above construction, or phrase, is so-called because it is ....

.... with the rest of the sentence. This is

indicated via punctuation by setting the phrase off with ....

3. The key test which the Romans applied for correctly using the above

construction was that its noun or pronoun could not also appear as

.... or .... of the verb in the main

clause.

4. Two nouns or a noun and an adjective in the ....

case can be used as an ablative absolute without a word for 'being'

because the verb SUM has no ....

5. Translating the Ablative Absolute literally often results in a clumsy, awkward English sentence. It is frequently better translated as an English subordinate clause beginning with a .... whose choice depends on the circumstance reflected in the rest of the sentence.

6. Five subordinating conjunctions which are commonly used to translate the Ablative Absolute are ...., ..., ..., ..., or ....

7. Up to this point in our study of Latin, the idea of obligation or necessity has been expressed in Latin by the verb .... (ought, must) followed by an .... If the latter were in the passive voice, the person accomplishing its action would be expressed by the ablative of ....

8. Another construction, which the Romans often used to express the idea of obligation or necessity in the passive voice, was composed of the passive future participle (learned in the last lesson; also called the gerundive) with the verb .... This construction goes by the name of ....

9. In the above construction, because the verb SUM is involved, the participle or gerundive functions as a .... and agrees in ...., ... and .... with the ....

10. Since the above construction is passive, one would expect that the

person accomplishing the action would be expressed by the ablative

of ....; but, with this construc-

tion, the Romans used instead a .... of ....

with no preposition.

CHAPTER XXIV

NAME _____ SECTION _____ DATE _____

II. DRILL.

  A. Supply the correct form of the words in parentheses and translate.

    a. .... (servus; capere, perfect passive participle),

    dūcēs urbem recēpērunt. ....

    ....

    b. Imperium ducī ....(quaerere, participle expressing

    necessity) est. ....

    c. .... (lībertās; recipere, perfect passive participle),

    servī pācem quaesīvērunt. ....

    ....

    d. Hominēs malī ducī ....(expellere, participle express-

    ing necessity) sunt. ....

    e. ....(spēs; relinquere, perfect passive participle),

    quisque fūgit. ....

  B. Translate the following, using participles wherever possible.

    a. When these things had been said, the leader accepted the gifts.

    ....

    b. That sign must be given to you.

    ....

    c. After the king had been banished, the senate made laws.

    ....

    d. These verses have to be written by a poet.

    ....

    e. Why did the command have to be abandoned by each person?

    ....

III.   PRACTICE SENTENCES. (Before translating each, read the Latin <u>aloud</u> twice.)

a. Bonīs virīs imperium tenentibus, rēs pūblica valēbit. ....

....

b. Omnī cupiditāte pecūniae glōriaeque ex animō expulsā, ille dux sē

vīcit. ....

....

c. Omnēs cīvēs istum tyrannum timēbant, quī expellendus erat. ....

....

d. Tyrannō superātō, cīvēs lībertātem et iūra recēpērunt. ....

....

e. Multīs gentibus victīs, tōtum mundum tenēre cupīvistī. ....

....

f. Servitūs omnis generis per tōtum mundum opprimenda est. ....

....

g. Omnia igitur iūra cīvibus magnā cūrā cōnservanda sunt. ....

....

h. Officiīs ā cīvibus relictīs, rēs pūblica in magnō perīculō erit.

....

....

i. Vēritās et virtūs omnibus virīs semper quaerendae sunt. ....

....

j. Vēritāte et virtūte quaesītīs, rēs pūblica cōnservāta est. ....

....

CHAPTER XXV

All Infinitives Active and Passive;
Indirect Statement.

OBJECTIVES:

1. To review the present active and passive infinitives and to learn in addition the perfect and future active infinitives and the perfect passive infinitive.

2. To learn how the Romans used the Latin infinitives in Indirect Statement.

I. GRAMMAR.
(MEMORIZE PARADIGMS AND VOCABULARY BY REPEATING THEM ALOUD!)

1. The final letter which identifies the active present infinitive

of a Latin verb is .... while that which identifies the

Passive present is ....

2. The active perfect infinitive of a Latin verb is composed of the

.... stem (from the .... principal part)

plus the ending ....

3. The perfect passive infinitive is composed of the ....

.... participle plus ...., the present

infinitive of SUM. The future active infinitive is composed of the

.... participle plus ....,

the present infinitive of SUM.

4. Is the future passive infinitive a common form? (Circle one.)

yes   no

5. Using the verbs indicated, complete the following chart of infinitives for each conjugation.

NARRĀRE

| | Active | | Passive | |
	Latin	English	Latin	English
Present	....	....	....	....
Perfect	....	....	....	....
Future	....	....	....	....

TERRĒRE

| | Active | | Passive | |
	Latin	English	Latin	English
Present	....	....	....	....
Perfect	....	....	....	....
Future	....	....	....	....

EXPELLERE

| | Active | | Passive | |
	Latin	English	Latin	English
Present	....	....	....	....
Perfect	....	....	....	....
Future	....	....	....	....

ACCIPERE

| | Active | | Passive | |
	Latin	English	Latin	English
Present	....	....	....	....
Perfect	....	....	....	....
Future	....	....	....	....

SCĪRE

	Active		Passive	
	Latin	English	Latin	English
Present	....	....	....	....
Perfect	....	....	....	....
Future	....	....	....	....

6. The participles which form the passive perfect infinitive and the
   active future infinitive with ESSE are in form considered as
   .... and, therefore, agree
   with the .... of the infinitive.

7. A direct statement is one that is made directly and could be placed
   in .... marks.

8. An indirect statement is one that is reported indirectly and, therefore, follows verbs of four main categories or types which are those
   of ...., ..., ..., and
   ....

9. List 6 Latin verbs which belong in the SAYING category.

   a. .... d. ....
   b. .... e. ....
   c. .... f. ....

10. List 4 Latin verbs which belong in the KNOWING category.

    a. .... c. ....
    b. .... d. ....

11. List 3 Latin verbs which belong in the THINKING category.

    a. .... c. ....
    b. ....

12. List 3 Latin verbs which belong in the PERCEIVING category.

    a. .... c. ....

    b. ....

13. Both of the following are examples of indirect statements. Sentence #a is the one most often encountered in English. The form which is always used in Latin is (Circle the letter.)

    a. I believe that he is brave.

    b. I believe him to be brave.

14. In Latin indirect discourse, the subject of the infinitive <u>is always expressed</u> and is always in the .... case. If that subject is a person represented by a pronoun and is the same person as the subject of the verb of saying, etc. in the main clause the .... personal pronoun is used. If the subject is a different person represented by a pronoun, then the .... personal pronoun is used.

15. The tense of the infinitive in indirect statement does not depend on the .... of the main verb but on the .... relative to the main verb.

16. Fill in the blanks with the correct infinitive of AMŌ.

    a. Dīcunt eum ....eam. (The time is 'past', or prior to that of the main verb).

    b. Dīcent eum ....eam. (The time is 'present', or contemporaneous, relative to that of the main verb).

    c. Dīxērunt eum .... eam. (The time is 'future', or subsequent to that of the main verb).

CHAPTER XXV

NAME _____ SECTION _____ DATE _____

II. DRILL.

A. Translate only the verbs which could introduce an indirect statement.

a. videō .... f. neglegō ....

b. nesciō .... g. ostendō ....

c. parō .... h. spērō ....

d. crēdō .... i. iungō ....

e. terreō .... j. putō ....

B. Translate the following into English or Latin.

a. movērī   f. to have been seen (fem. acc. plu.)

....

b. crēdidisse   g. to be about to change (masc. acc.

.... sing.) ....

c. trāctōs esse   h. to be known

....

d. dīcī   i. to have touched

....

e. sustulisse   j. to have been sought (neuter acc.

.... sing.) ....

C. Supply the correct form of the words in parentheses and translate.

a. Negāvit adulēscentem .... (esse, same time) fīlium

suum. ....

b. Crēdō mē imperium ....(relinquere, time after).

....

c. Senātus nūntiāvit hostēs ....(venīre, time before).

....

d. Servī dīcent sē hīc .... (capere, passive, time before).

....

e. Vidēbimus dōna .... (dare, passive, same time).

....

D. Translate the following.

a. I know that he will come.

....

b. They believed that he had sent gifts.

....

c. You will see that the school is prepared.

....

d. The people related that they had been warned.

....

e. We believe that the human soul is immortal.

....

III. PRACTICE SENTENCES. (Before translating each, read the Latin <u>aloud</u> twice.)

a. Spērant vōs eum vīsūrōs esse. ....

....

b. Sciō hoc ā tē factum esse. ....

....

c. Nescīvī illa ab eō facta esse. ....

....

d. Putābant tyrannum sibi expellendum esse. ....

....

e. Crēdimus pācem omnibus ducibus quaerendam esse. ....

....

f. Hostēs nostrī crēdunt omnem rem pūblicam sibi vincendam esse. ....

....

g. Hostēs spērant sē omnēs rēs pūblicās victūrōs esse. ....

....

h. Bene sciō mē multa nescīre; nēmō enim potest omnia scīre. ....

....

CHAPTER XXVI

Comparison of Adjectives;
Declension of Comparatives.

OBJECTIVE:

To learn how to form the comparative and superlative degree of adjectives in Latin and how to decline the two new forms.

I. GRAMMAR.
(MEMORIZE PARADIGMS AND VOCABULARY BY REPEATING THEM ALOUD!)

1. The Latin adjective CLĀRUS, -A, -UM means ....

2. The comparative of CLĀRUS is ....

for which four translations are possible: ....,

...., ...

or ....

3. The comparative form of Latin adjectives is declined like the

.... adjectives of the .... declension,

except that the comparatives have .... stems and do not

show the characteristic -i- of the third declension adjectives in three

places: ...., ..., and

....

4. The Latin adverb MAGIS is used with the positive degree of certain

adjectives to form the comparative degree when a ....

precedes the endings of those adjectives.

5. The Latin conjunction QUAM <u>after</u> a comparative adjective means

.... and the word or idea (or second member) following

it has .... as the corresponding word or idea

(or first member) before the conjunction.

6. The superlative of CLĀRUS is ...., for
    which three translations are possible: ...., or
    .... or ....

7. The superlative form of Latin adjectives is declined like ....
    ....

8. The Latin adverb MAXIMĒ is used with the positive degree of certain
    adjectives to form the superlative degree when a ....
    precedes the endings of those adjectives.

9. The Latin conjunction QUAM <u>before</u> the superlative adjective
    FORTISSIMUS means ....

10. Complete the following:

<u>Positive</u>	<u>Comparative</u>	<u>Superlative</u>
POTĒNS, -ENTIS	....	....
IŪCUNDUS, -A, -UM	....	....
PERPETUUS, -A, -UM	....	....
DULCIS, -E	....	....
SAPIĒNS, -ENTIS	....	....

CHAPTER XXVI

NAME _____ SECTION _____ DATE _____

II. DRILL.

A. Translate the following into English or Latin.

a. iūcundiōrēs (acc.)

....

b. gravissimum (nom.)

....

c. breviōribus (abl.)

....

d. turpiōra (nom.)

....

e. difficiliōris

....

f. incertissimīs (dat.)

....

g. commūnius (acc.)

....

h. magis idōneō (dat.)

....

i. fidēlissimī (sing.)

....

j. vēriōrum

....

k. too short (acc. masc. sing.)

....

l. as long as possible (gen. neut. sing.) ....

m. happier (nom. neut. sing.)

....

n. most suitable (acc. neut. plu.)

....

o. very uncertain (abl. masc. sing.)

....

p. rather bitter (dat. fem. plu.)

....

q. more serious (acc. neut. sing.)

....

r. sweetest (gen. fem. plu.)

....

s. dearer (gen. fem. plu.)

....

t. wiser (abl. masc. sing.)

....

B. Supply the correct form of the words in parentheses and translate.

a. Vītā .... (potēns, comparative) lūcem.

....

b. Auctor scrīpsit versūs .... (acerbus, superlative).

....

c. Memoria lūcis .... (clārus, superlative) remānsit.

....

d. Crēdō eam esse ....(fidēlis, comparative) quam eum.

....

e. Hostis quam ....(brevis, superlative) litterās mittet.

....

C. Translate the following.

a. Send men as wise as possible.

....

b. You will read a rather short book.

....

c. Nothing is more certain than death.

....

d. The danger is too serious for me.

....

e. The most pleasant memories always remain.

....

III. PRACTICE SENTENCES. (Before translating each, read the Latin aloud twice.)

a. Nūntiāvērunt ducem quam fortissimum vēnisse. ....

....

b. Lūce clārissimā ab omnibus vīsā, cōpiae fortissimae contrā hostēs

missae sunt. ....

....

c. Istō homine turpissimō expulsō, senātus cīvibus fidēliōribus dōna

dedit. ....

....

d. Hic auctor est clārior quam ille. ....

....

e. Quīdam dīxērunt hunc auctōrem esse clāriōrem quam illum. ....

....

f. Quibusdam librīs sapientissimīs lēctīs, illa vitia turpiōra vītāvimus.

....

....

g. Quis est vir fēlīcissimus? ....

h. Remedium vitiōrum vestrōrum vidētur difficilius. ....

....

i. Ille dux putāvit patriam esse sibi cāriōrem quam vītam. ....

....

j. Manus adulēscentium quam fidēlissimōrum senātuī quaerenda est. ......

....

....

CHAPTER XXVII

Special and Irregular Comparison of Adjectives.

OBJECTIVES:

1. To learn to form the special superlatives of adjectives ending in -LIS and -ER.

2. To identify and memorize the few frequently encountered Latin adjectives whose comparison is completely irregular.

3. To learn the peculiarities of the declension of PLŪS.

I. GRAMMAR.
   (MEMORIZE PARADIGMS AND VOCABULARY BY REPEATING THEM ALOUD!)

   1. List the six adjectives ending in -LIS whose superlative is peculiar in form, and compare them below.

Positive	Comparative	Superlative
....	....	....
....	....	....
....	....	....
....	....	....
....	....	....
....	....	....

   2. Give three examples of adjectives having a masculine ending of the positive degree in -ER which form the superlative in a special way, and compare them below.

Positive	Comparative	Superlative
....	....	....
....	....	....
....	....	....

3. Give the Latin comparatives and superlatives from which the following
    English words are derived (write underneath each), and list the
    corresponding positive degree of the Latin word.

Positive	Comparative	Superlative
	pejorative	pessimist
....	....	....
	prior	primary
....	....	....
	superiority	summit and supremacy
....	....	....
	minority	minimize
....	....	....
	majority	maximum
....	....	....
	ameliorate	optimist
....	....	....

4. The English expression MORE OF (SOMETHING) is translated by the Latin
    neuter noun PLUS which logically governs the genitive case. It is
    used for the comparative of MULTUS meaning MUCH. It is always
    singular and is declined as follows:

    Nom ....

    Gen ....

    Dat ....

    Acc ....

    Abl ....

5. The plural of PLŪS is used for the comparative of MULTĪ meaning MANY.
   It is an adjective and is declined as follows:

	M + F	N
Nom	....	....
Gen	....	....
Dat	....	....
Acc	....	....
Abl	....	....

CHAPTER XXVII

NAME _____ SECTION _____ DATE _____

II. DRILL.

    A. Translate the following into English or Latin.

        a. bellum maius   k. the best author

        ....

        b. liber simillimus   l. the most beautiful sun

        ....

        c. puer minimus   m. a more difficult book

        ....

        d. puella pulcherrima   n. the very easy verses

        ....

        e. frūctus peior   o. rather difficult work

        ....

        f. plūs labōris   p. a freer people

        ....

        g. plūrēs labōrēs   q. the worst reasons

         ....

        h. dōna prīma   r. the last day

        ....

        i. cīvēs pessimī   s. a greater friendship

        ....

        j. plūs laudis   t. the highest heavens

        ....

    B. Supply the correct form of the words in parentheses and translate.

        a. Lūx sōlis .... (bonus, superlative) est.

        ....

b. .... (celer, superlative) remedium non semper ....

(magnus, superlative) est. ....

c. ....(sapiēns, comparative) virī saepe ....

(parvus, comparative) numerum librōrum scrībunt. ....

....

d. Maiōrēs ex adulēscentibus ....(multus, comparative,

acc. sing.) exspectābant. ....

e. Senectūs .... (difficilis, comparative) aetās est.

....

C. Translate the following.

a. His son was older than his daughter.

....

b. The daughter was more beautiful than her mother.

....

c. Our ancestors called the sun a god.

....

d. The greatest friendships are often the most difficult.

....

e. More authors were writing about their own land.

....

III. PRACTICE SENTENCES. (Before translating each, read the Latin _aloud_ twice.)

a. Facillima saepe nōn sunt optima. ....

....

b. Difficilia saepe sunt maxima. ....

....

c. Meliōra studia sunt difficiliōra. ....

....

d. Puer minor maius dōnum accēpit. ....

....

e. Plūrēs virī crēdunt hoc bellum esse peius quam prīmum bellum. ....

....

f. Dux melior cum cōpiīs maiōribus veniet. ....

....

g. Meliōrī ducī maius imperium et plūs pecūniae dedērunt. ....

....

h. Cīvēs urbium minōrum nōn sunt meliōrēs quam eī urbium maximārum. ....

....

i. Nōs nōn meliōrēs sumus quam plūrimī virī priōrum aetātum. ....

....

j. Maiōrēs nostrī Apollinem (Apollō, acc.) deum sōlis appellābant. ....

....

CHAPTER XXVIII

Subjunctive:
Present Active and Passive;
Jussive; Purpose.

OBJECTIVES:

1. To understand the idea underlying the Latin subjunctive mood.

2. To learn the conjugation of the active and passive present subjunctive in all conjugations.

3. To understand the basic principle governing the translation of Latin subjunctive situations.

4. To begin to master the use of the subjunctive by learning two situations which require it: the jussive (command idea) in independent clauses, and purpose in subordinate clauses.

I. GRAMMAR.
(MEMORIZE PARADIGMS AND VOCABULARY BY REPEATING THEM ALOUD!)

1. The indicative mood is employed to express ....

   (see W. p. 1 n. 1).

2. The subjunctive mood can be employed to express ....,

   ...., etc.

3. The English subjunctive is used (Circle one.)

   rarely   frequently

4. The Latin subjunctive is used (Circle one.)

   rarely   frequently

5. The Latin present subjunctive is formed in the first conjugation by

   changing the present stem vowel -a- to .... and adding

   the .... or .... personal endings.

   In the three other conjugations, the vowel .... is

   consistently the sign of the present subjunctive active and passive.

6. Conjugate the following verbs as indicated:

Subjunctive Present

		Active			Passive	
		AMĀRE	VIDĒRE	MITTERE	RAPERE	INVENĪRE
Singular	1.	....	....	....	....	....
	2.	....	....	....	....	....
	3.	....	....	....	....	....
Plural	1.	....	....	....	....	....
	2.	....	....	....	....	....
	3.	....	....	....	....	....

7. Since there is no standard translation into English for the Latin subjunctive, one must be fashioned to reproduce its various ideas according to the ....

8. The most prominent use of the subjunctive in independent, or main, clauses is to express the idea of a ....

9. The above idea is rendered in Latin in the first person by using what is called the ...., in the second person by the ...., and in the third person by the ....

10. In English, the subordinate clause of purpose is usually expressed by the ...., while Latin employs the .... mood.

11. The conjunctions which introduce Latin purpose clauses are .... for the positive and .... for the negative.

CHAPTER XXVIII

NAME _____ SECTION _____ DATE _____

II. DRILL.

A. Translate the indicative verb forms and label the subjunctives by
   person and number.

   a. audīmur   k. audiāmur

   ....

   b. sciantur   l. līberāminī

   ....

   c. iubeam   m. acciperis (-re)

   ....

   d. līberābiminī   n. appellētis

   ....

   e. mittit   o. sciuntur

   ....

   f. scientur   p. mittet

   ....

   g. accipiēris (-re)   q. iubear

   ....

   h. appellātis   r. iubēbar

   ....

   i. līberēminī   s. accipiāris (-re)

   ....

   j. audiēmur   t. mittat

   ....

B. Supply the correct form of the verbs in parentheses and translate.

   a. Nē arma ....(praestāre, 1st person plural, sub-

   junctive). ....

b. Lībertātis causā verbum suum ....(dare, 3rd person

plural, subjunctive). ....

c. Ōrātōrem ....(audīre, 1st person plural, subjunctive)

ut in pāce ....(vīvere, 1st person plural).

....

d. Cīvēs pessimōs expellāmus nē optimī insidiās ....

(timēre, 3rd person plural). ....

....

e. Beneficia amīcitiae ....(laudāre, 1st person singular,

subjunctive). ....

C. Translate the following.

a. Let him send us arms.

....

b. They come to offer better arms. (See W. p. 133 and n. 4)

....

c. Let us avoid the danger of war.

....

d. He writes those words in order that he may help the people.

....

e. Let her read the letter in order that she may not flee.

....

III. PRACTICE SENTENCES. (Before translating each, read the Latin aloud twice.)

a. Ille dux veniat. Eum exspectāmus. ....

....

b. Beneficia aliīs praestat ut amētur. ....

....

c. Haec verba fēlīcia vōbīs dīcō nē discēdātis. ....

....

d. Patriae causā haec difficillima faciāmus. ....

....

e. Arma parēmus nē lībertās nostra tollātur. ....

....

f. Armīsne sōlīs lībertās nostra ē perīculō ēripiētur? ....

....

g. Nē sapientēs librōs difficiliōrēs scrībant. ....

....

h. Sapientiam enim ā librīs difficiliōribus nōn accipiēmus. ....

....

i. Meliōra et maiōra faciat nē vītam miserrimam agat. ....

....

j. Haec illī auctōrī clarissimō nārrā ut in librō eius scrībantur. .....

....

....

CHAPTER XXIX

Imperfect Subjunctive;
Present and Imperfect Subjunctive of SUM;
Result.

OBJECTIVES:

1. To learn the conjugation of the active and passive Latin imperfect subjunctive tense in all conjugations.

2. To learn the present and imperfect subjunctive of ESSE and POSSE.

3. To understand the use of the imperfect subjunctive tense.

4. To learn the second situation in Latin subordinate clauses which governs the subjunctive: that of result.

I. GRAMMAR.
    (MEMORIZE PARADIGMS AND VOCABULARY BY REPEATING THEM ALOUD!)

    1. The imperfect subjunctive, in all four regular Latin conjugations, is

        formed by combining, as a stem, the ....

        ...., or the

        .... principal part of a verb, with the ....

        .... or .... personal endings.

    2. Conjugate the following verbs as indicated.

Subjunctive Imperfect

		Passive			Active	
		APPELLĀRE	MOVĒRE	VINCERE	IACERE	SENTĪRE
	1.	....	....	....	....	....
Singular	2.	....	....	....	....	....
	3.	....	....	....	....	....
	1.	....	....	....	....	....
Plural	2.	....	....	....	....	....
	3.	....	....	....	....	....

3. Conjugate the following:

Subjunctive

		Present		Imperfect	
		ESSE	POSSE	ESSE	POSSE
Singular	1.	....	....	....	....
	2.	....	....	....	....
	3.	....	....	....	....
Plural	1.	....	....	....	....
	2.	....	....	....	....
	3.	....	....	....	....

4. The imperfect subjunctive has no standard English translation. The Romans used it in purpose clauses and in result clauses when the main verb was in a .... tense.

5. In Latin sentences which include purpose or result clauses, the mood of the main verb can be ...., ..., or ....

6. When Latin purpose or result clauses are positive, the conjunction which introduces either one is ....

7. When Latin purpose or result clauses are negative, the conjunction which introduces a purpose clause is .... and that which introduces a result clause is ....

8. In Latin sentences, the presence of a result clause can often be determined by the following three indicator words found in the principal clause:

	Latin Word	Meaning
a.	....	....
b.	....	....
c.	....	....

CHAPTER XXIX

NAME _____ SECTION _____ DATE _____

II. DRILL.

  A. Translate the indicative verb forms and label the subjunctives by
      number, person and tense.

      a. vocāret   k. posset

      ....

      b. vidērēmus   l. vidēmus

      ....

      c. expellēminī   m. discēderent

      ....

      d. ēriperēs   n. discēdant

      ....

      e. servārētis   o. possīmus

      ....

      f. inveniēs   p. accipiās

      ....

      g. possumus   q. ēripiēs

      ....

      h. dīcat   r. acciperēs

      ....

      i. dīcit   s. expellerēminī

      ....

      j. moventur   t. movērentur

      ....

  B. Supply the correct form of the verbs in parentheses and translate.

      a. Discipulī tantōs librōs lēgērunt ut vēritātem ....

      (discere, 3rd person plural). ....

      ....

b. Auctor tam bene scrīpsit ut omnēs librōs eius ....

(legere, 1st person plural). ....

....

c. Adulēscēns tam dūrus erat ut amīcōs nōn .... (habēre,

3rd person singular). ....

....

d. Tanta dīxit ut imperium tibi .... (dare, 1st person

plural). ....

....

e. Hic lūdus ita bonus est ut multa .... (discere, 1st

person singular). ....

....

C. Translate the following.

a. The sign was so clear that everyone saw it.

....

b. The laws are so harsh that there is no liberty.

....

c. He helped them with arms so that the city might not be conquered.

....

d. He wrote so well that the students learned his verses.

....

e. You have such a great mind that you are able to learn many things.

....

III. PRACTICE SENTENCES. (Before translating each, read the Latin aloud twice.)

a. Bonōs librōs cum cūrā legēbāmus ut sapientiam discerēmus. ....

....

b. Optimī librī discipulīs legendī sunt ut vēritātem et mōrēs bonōs

discant. ....

....

c. Animī plūrimōrum hominum tam stultī sunt ut discere nōn cupiant. ....

....

d. At multae mentēs ita ācrēs sunt ut bene discere possint. ....

....

e. Omnēs cīvēs sē patriae dent nē hostēs lībertātem tollant. ....

....

....

f. Caesar tam ācer dux erat ut hostēs mīlitēs Rōmānōs nōn vincerent. ...

....

....

g. Tanta beneficia faciēbātis ut omnēs vōs amārent. ....

....

h. Tam dūrus erat ut nēmō eum amāret. ....

....

i. Multī cīvēs ex eā terrā fugiēbant nē ā tyrannō opprimerentur. ......

....

....

j. Lībertātem sīc amāvērunt ut numquam ab hostibus vincerentur. ....

....

....

CHAPTER XXX

Perfect and Pluperfect Subjunctive Active and Passive;
Indirect Questions;
Sequence of Tenses.

OBJECTIVES:

1. To learn the conjugation of the active and passive Latin perfect and pluperfect subjunctive tenses in all conjugations.

2. To review direct and indirect statements (Chapter XXV), to contrast them with direct and indirect questions, and to learn the third situation in Latin subordinate clauses which requires the subjunctive: that of indirect question.

3. To identify the indicative and subjunctive tenses which belong to the two groups known as PRIMARY and HISTORICAL (or SECONDARY) and to learn and apply the basic rule for the use of Latin tenses called SEQUENCE OF TENSES.

I. GRAMMAR.
   (MEMORIZE PARADIGMS AND VOCABULARY BY REPEATING THEM ALOUD!)

   1. Comparing the structure of the active perfect and pluperfect subjunctive tenses, one can see that both are constructed from the .... stem plus the respective tense signs .... and .... and the active personal endings.

   2. Comparing the structure of the passive perfect and pluperfect subjunctive tenses, one can see that both are constructed from the perfect passive .... plus the .... or .... subjunctive of the verb ESSE.

3. Using the verbs indicated, conjugate the following:

Subjunctive

		Perfect		Pluperfect		
		MUTĀRE	MOVĒRE	TRAHERE	IACERE	INVENĪRE

Active

		MUTĀRE	MOVĒRE	TRAHERE	IACERE	INVENĪRE
	1.	....	....	....	....	....
Singular	2.	....	....	....	....	....
	3.	....	....	....	....	....
	1.	....	....	....	....	....
Plural	2.	....	....	....	....	....
	3.	....	....	....	....	....

Passive

		MUTĀRE	MOVĒRE	TRAHERE	IACERE	INVENĪRE
	1.	....	....	....	....	....
Singular	2.	....	....	....	....	....
	3.	....	....	....	....	....
	1.	....	....	....	....	....
Plural	2.	....	....	....	....	....
	3.	....	....	....	....	....

4. In Latin and in English, verbs in a principal clause which precedes an indirect question are those of ...., ..., ... and .... The word which introduces the indirect question of the subordinate clause is an .... word. The verb of indirect questions, in Latin, is in the .... mood.

5. The following chart is designed to illustrate the Roman way of
    designating tenses as PRIMARY or HISTORICAL (SECONDARY) and the basic
    rule, called SEQUENCE OF TENSES, for the use of those tenses in Latin.
    Fill in the appropriate tenses of the subjunctive (note that you must
    determine whether the action indicated by the verb in the subordinate
    clause occurs before, after, or at the same time as the action of the
    verb in the principal clause):

<u>MAIN CLAUSES</u>   <u>SUBORDINATE CLAUSES</u>

(Indicative, Imperative,   (Subjunctive)
or Jussive Subjunctive)

<u>PRIMARY TENSES</u>   Present or Future time   ....(for simultaneous
                    (plus perfect for English   or subsequent time)
                    present perfect)
                                                  ....(for prior time)

<u>HISTORICAL TENSES</u> Past time   ....(for simultaneous
   (SECONDARY)   or subsequent time)

                                                  ....(for prior time)

6. Therefore, the basic rule for SEQUENCE OF TENSES, simply stated, is

    that a .... tense of the subjunctive is always

    used with a .... tense of the main verb and a

    .... tense of the subjunctive is always used

    with a .... tense of the main verb.

CHAPTER XXX

NAME _____ SECTION _____ DATE _____

II. DRILL.

A. Give the voice, person, number and tense of each of the following
subjunctive forms.

a. iusserim   k. amāverīs

....

b. posueritis   l. iussissem

....

c. amārēs   m. scītus sim

....

d. rapiāminī   n. posuissētis

....

e. scīvissem   o. amārēris (-re)

....

f. iussus essem   p. raperēminī

....

g. rapiāmus   q. scītus essem

....

h. pōnerētis   r. scīverim

....

i. amēris (-re)   s. positī essētis

....

j. raperēmus   t. iussus sim

....

B. Supply the correct form of the verbs in parentheses and translate.

a. Rogāvit ubi ferra .... (invenīre, passive, time prior).

....

b. Mundus rogat unde malum ....(venīre, active, time

contemporaneous). ....

c. Ducēs comprehendent cūr ....(fugere, 1st person plural,

active, time prior). ....

....

d. Discesseram ut sōlem ....(vītāre, 1st person singular,

active, time contemporaneous). ....

....

e. Pater meus exposuit cūr ....(discēdere, 1st person

singular, active, time prior). ....

....

C. Translate the following:

a. We learned so much that we arrested the speaker.

....

b. We will learn why the speaker has been arrested.

....

c. The general asked whence the soldiers had come.

....

d. He will ask when the sword was placed there.

....

e. You know why the signal has not been given.

....

III. PRACTICE SENTENCES. (Before translating each, read the Latin aloud twice.)

a. Nesciō ubi pecūnia posita sit. ....

b. Scīsne ubi pecūnia ponātur? ....

c. Scīvērunt ubi pecūnia ponerētur. ....

....

d. Nescīvit ubi pecūnia posita esset. ....

....

e. Ōrātor rogāvit cūr cēterī cīvēs haec cōnsilia nōn cognōvissent. .....

....

f. Audīvimus cīvēs tam fidēlēs esse ut rem pūblicam cōnservārent. ......

....

g. Audīvimus quid cīvēs fēcissent ut rem pūblicam cōnservārent. ....

....

h. Quaerēbant quōrum in rē pūblicā pāx invenīrī posset. ....

....

i. Cognōvimus pācem in patriā eōrum nōn inventam esse. ....

....

j. Illī stultī semper rogant quid sit melius quam imperium aut pecūnia.

....

....

CHAPTER XXXI

CUM with the Subjunctive;
FERŌ.

OBJECTIVES:

1. To learn a fourth situation in Latin subordinate clauses which usually
    requires the subjunctive: that involving the conjunction CUM.

2. To learn the principal parts of the irregular verb FERRE and those few
    forms which omit the connecting E or I and do not follow the 3rd conju-
    gation paradigm of DŪCERE.

I. GRAMMAR.
    (MEMORIZE PARADIGMS AND VOCABULARY BY REPEATING THEM ALOUD!)

    1. Before this chapter, we considered the Latin word CUM to be a

        .... whose English meaning is ....

    2. The Romans also used the word CUM at the beginning of a subordinate

        clause as a conjunction which, when followed by the subjunctive, had

        three basic meanings: .... when past circumstances

        of an event were emphasized, ... when the cause of

        something was indicated, and .... which indicated a

        concession and was commonly accompanied by the word ....

        in the main clause.

    3. The four principal parts of the Latin irregular verb FERRE are:

        ....

    4. In addition to the obviously irregular perfect and participial forms

        of FERRE, the basic reason for its irregularity in other tenses is

        lack of the connecting vowels .... or .... Other-

        wise, FERRE belongs to the .... conjugation and is

        conjugated like ....

5. Conjugate the following tenses of FERRE:

		Indicative		Imperative	Infinitive	
		Present		Present	Present	
		Active	Passive	Active	Active	Passive
Singular	1.	....	....		....	....
	2.	....	....	....		
	3.	....	....			
Plural	1.	....	....			
	2.	....	....	....		
	3.	....	....			

CHAPTER XXXI

NAME _____ SECTION _____ DATE _____

II. DRILL.

A. Label the subjunctives by voice, person, number and tense and translate the remaining forms:

a. tulisse

....

b. lātūrus esse

....

c. ferendus

....

d. lātus esse

....

e. tulisset

....

f. fertis

....

g. ferēris (-re)

....

h. ferris (-re)

....

i. fer

....

j. ferrī

....

k. ferunt

....

l. ferent

....

m. ferant

....

n. fertur

....

o. ferte

....

p. ferat

....

q. fert

....

q. ferret

....

s. feret

....

k. lātus eram

....

B. Supply the correct form of the verbs in parentheses and translate.

    a. Cum mediocris .... (esse, 3rd person singular, time prior), tamen eum tolerāmus. ....

    ....

    b. Cum in exsilium .... (mittere, passive, 3rd person plural, time contemporaneous), nullum auxilium datum est. ....

    ....

    c. Cum vīnum tibi ....(dare, passive, time contemporaneous), tamen exsilium nōn bene fers. ....

    ....

    d. Cum apud hostēs ....(esse, 2nd person plural, time contemporaneous), amīcī sē ad vōs nāve contulērunt. ....

    ....

    e. Cum auxilium ....(ferre, 3rd person plural, time prior), unō annō hoc fēcimus. ....

    ....

C. Translate the following.

    a. Although the times were calm, swords were nevertheless carried.

    ....

    b. When the exile of the leader had been ordered, they departed.

    ....

    c. Because the opportunities were few, the ships were prepared.

    ....

    d. Since the students had been thrown out, they came to the teacher's house. ....

    ....

    e. When the ship departs, the seas will be moderate.

    ....

III. PRACTICE SENTENCES.   (Before translating each, read the Latin <u>aloud</u> twice)

a. Cum hoc dīxissēmus, illī respondērunt sē pācem aequam oblātūrōs esse.

....

....

b. Cum sē in aliam terram contulisset, tamen amīcōs novōs invēnit. ......

....

c. Cum amīcitiam nōbīs offerant, eīs auxilium offerēmus. ....

....

d. Cum perīculum magnum esset, omnēs cōpiās et arma brevī tempore

cōntulērunt. ....

....

e. Cum exposuisset quid peteret, negāvistī tantum auxilium posse offerrī.

....

....

f. Cum dōna iūcunda tulissent, potuī tamen īnsidiās eōrum cognōscere. ..

....

....

g. Cum cōnsilia tua nunc comprehendāmus, īnsidiās tuās nōn ferēmus. ....

....

....

h. Cum mīlitēs nostrī hostēs vīcissent, tamen eīs multa beneficia

obtulērunt. ....

....

i. Cum cognōvisset quanta beneficia cēterī offerrent, ipse aequa

beneficia obtulit. ....

....

j. Cum consul haec verba dīxisset, senātus respondit pecūniam ad hanc

rem collātam esse. ....

....

CHAPTER XXXII

Adverbs: Formation and Comparison;
VOLŌ.

OBJECTIVES:

1. To learn how to construct and compare regular Latin adverbs.

2. To know the positive, comparative and superlative forms of the most often encountered irregular Latin adverbs.

3. To learn the principal parts and the irregular forms of the Latin irregular verb VELLE and of its derivatives NŌLLE and MĀLLE.

I. GRAMMAR.
    (MEMORIZE PARADIGMS AND VOCABULARY BY REPEATING THEM ALOUD!)

  1. Review the comparison of adjectives in Chapters XXVI and XXVII.

  2. Regular Latin adverbs are formed, in the positive degree, by dropping the ending of the adjective and adding to the base, for declension 1/2, the ending .... and, for declension 3, the ending .... Both of these correspond to the English adverbial ending ....

  3. Regular Latin adverbs of 3rd declension adjectives whose base ends in -NT- do not follow the above but are simply formed by adding .... to the base.

  4. The comparative of regular Latin adverbs uses the ending .... which makes the adverb identical with the comparative degree .... ending form of the Latin adjective. In English the comparative degree of an adverb is usually formed by placing the word .... before the positive adverb. Two other words sometimes useful in translating the Latin comparative are .... and ....

5. The superlative of regular Latin adverbs is formed by dropping the ending of the superlative degree of an adjective and adding to the base the ending .... In English the superlative degree of an adverb is usually formed by placing the words .... or .... before the positive adverb.

6. List ten Latin adverbs having special, individual forms (along with their English meanings) which we have already learned in our vocabulary (e.g. iam, already):

Latin	English	Latin	English
a)	....	f)	....
b)	....	g)	....
c)	....	h)	....
d)	....	i)	....
e)	....	j)	....

7. The comparison of irregular Latin adverbs usually follows the basic .... of the adjective.

8. The two Latin irregular verbs which are compounds of VELLE are .... and .... which, broken down, are .... and .... and whose meanings are .... and ....

CHAPTER XXXII

NAME _____ SECTION _____ DATE _____

II. DRILL.

A. Translate the following adverbs into English or Latin.

a. iūcundē ....   f. least ....

b. fidēlissimē ....   g. longer ....

c. breviter ....   h. badly ....

d. peius ....   i. less ....

e. fidēlius ....   j. fastest ....

B. Label the subjunctives by person, number, and tense, and translate the remaining forms.

a. volēs   f. velīmus

....

b. vultis   g. vellēmus

....

c. vīs   h. voluissēs

....

d. volunt   i. voluistī

....

e. vult   j. vellet

....

C. Supply the correct form of the words in parentheses and translate.

a. Custōdiae .... (celer, adverb, superlative) sē mōvērunt.

....

b. Lēgēs habēre ....(sapiēns, adverb, positive) māluimus.

....

c. Auctor aut dīvitiās aut honōrēs ....(vērus, adverb, positive) vītāre voluerat. ....

....

d. Exercitū eius ....(facilis, adverb, superlative) victī sumus. ....

....

e. Dīvitēs plūrēs dīvitiās ....(celer, adverb, comparative) habēre volent. ....

....

D. Translate the following.

a. They took the wealth very happily.

....

b. Our students will learn more quickly.

....

c. The law was rather badly read.

....

d. Words are often harshly spoken.

....

e. Knowledge must always be most clearly understood.

....

III. PRACTICE SENTENCES. (Before translating each, read the Latin aloud twice.)

a. Quīdam volunt crēdere omnēs hominēs esse pārēs. ....

....

b. Quīdam negant mentēs quidem omnium hominum esse pārēs. ....

....

c. Hī dīvitiās celerrimē invēnērunt; illī diūtissimē erunt pauperēs. ...

....

....

d. Hic plūrimōs honōrēs quam facillimē accipere vult. ....

....

e. Nōs maximē volumus scientiam quaerere. ....

....

f. Cīvēs ipsī rem pūblicam melius gessērunt quam ille dux. ....

....

g. Ibi terra est aequior et plūs patet. ....

....

h. Tyrannus cīvēs suōs ita male opprimēbat ut semper līberī esse vellent.

....

....

i. Plūrima dōna līberrimē offeret ut exercitus istum tyrannum adiuvāre

velit. ....

....

j. Vult haec sapientius facere nē hanc quidem occasiōnem āmittat. ......

....

....

CHAPTER XXXIII

Conditions.

OBJECTIVE:

To learn the table of conditions in order to know the moods and tenses
and, therefore, the correct meaning of the various forms of the basic
Latin conditional sentences.

I. GRAMMAR.
    (MEMORIZE PARADIGMS AND VOCABULARY BY REPEATING THEM ALOUD!)

1. Conditional sentences in English and in Latin include a subordinate

    clause called the .... which begins in

    Latin with the conjunction........................ for the positive,

    meaning...................., and .... for the

    negative, meaning .... They also

    include a main clause called the ....

2. The table below represents another possible way of cataloguing
    Latin conditional sentences according to the mood of the verbs.
    Note the basic division into two groups (above and below the solid
    line). The group above the line with the indicative implies certainty
    or hard fact (See W. p. 1 n. 1). The group below the line with the
    subjunctive implies situations that are merely hypothetical or quite
    contrary to fact (i.e., unrealizable). Give the correct tense(s) to
    be used for each type of condition.

INDICATIVE MOOD (<u>Simple</u> <u>Fact</u>)

	<u>Conditional Clause</u>	<u>Main Clause (Conclusion)</u>
1. Present time	....	....
2. Past time	.... or	.... or ....
3. Future more vivid	.... or	....

SUBJUNCTIVE MOOD (<u>Hypothetical</u> or <u>Unrealizable</u>)

1. Future less vivid	....	....
2. Present contrary to fact	....	....
3. Past contrary to fact	....	....

3. In the <u>conditional</u> clause of the <u>future more vivid</u> above, Latin more logically has the .... tense where English regularly has the .... tense.

4. The future less vivid condition is nicknamed the .... condition.

CHAPTER XXXIII

NAME _____ SECTION _____ DATE _____

II. DRILL.

  A. Supply the correct form of the verb in parentheses and translate.

    a. (Future less vivid, should/would) SĪ hoc ....(legere, 2nd person plural), ...(discere, 2nd person plural).

    ....

    b. (Contrary to fact, past) SĪ hoc............(legere, 2nd person plural), ...(discere, 2nd person plural).

    ....

    c. (Simple fact, past) SĪ hoc ....(legere, 2nd person plural), ...(discere, 2nd person plural).

    ....

    d. (Contrary to fact, present) SĪ hoc ....(legere, 2nd person plural), ...(discere, 2nd person plural).

    ....

    e. (Future more vivid) SĪ hoc ....(legere, 2nd person plural), ...(discere, 2nd person plural).

    ....

  B. Translate the following.

    a. If you undertake the thing, you will surrender safety.

    ....

    b. If you should undertake the thing, you would surrender safety.

    ....

    c. If you had undertaken the thing, you would have surrendered safety.

    ....

    d.   If you undertook the thing, you surrendered safety.

....

    e.   If you were undertaking the thing, you would surrender safety.

....

III.   PRACTICE SENTENCES. (Before translating each, read the Latin <u>aloud</u> twice.)

    a.   Sī ratiō dūcit, fēlīx es. ....

....

    b.   Sī ratiō dūcet, fēlīx eris. ....

....

    c.   Sī ratiō dūcat, fēlīx sīs. ....

....

    d.   Sī ratiō dūceret, fēlīx essēs. ....

....

    e.   Sī ratiō dūxisset, fēlīx fuissēs. ....

....

    f.   Sī pecūniam amās, sapientiā carēs. ....

....

    g.   Sī pecūniam amābis, sapientiā carēbis. ....

....

    h.   Sī pecūniam amēs, sapientiā careās. ....

....

    i.   Sī pecūniam amārēs, sapientiā carērēs. ....

....

    j.   Sī pecūniam amāvissēs, sapientiā caruissēs. ....

....

    k.   Sī vēritātem quaerimus, scientiam invenīmus. ....

....

1. Sī vēritātem quaerēmus, scientiam inveniēmus. ....

....

m. Sī vēritātem quaerāmus, scientiam inveniāmus. ....

....

n. Sī vēritātem quaererēmus, scientiam invenīrēmus. ....

....

o. Sī vēritātem quaesīvissēmus, scientiam invēnissēmus. ....

....

CHAPTER XXXIV

Deponent Verbs;
Ablative with Special Deponents.

OBJECTIVES:

1. To learn the regular forms of Latin deponent verbs as well as the peculiarities of their participles, infinitives and imperatives.

2. To learn representative Latin semi-deponent verbs.

3. To learn representative Latin special deponent verbs which govern the ablative (of means) because they are really reflexive verbs.

I. GRAMMAR.
   (MEMORIZE PARADIGMS AND VOCABULARY BY REPEATING THEM ALOUD!)

   1. Latin deponent verbs are so named from the Latin verb DĒ-PŌNŌ which

      means .... This term 'deponent' indicates

      that the Latin .... forms have been 'laid aside' for

      .... meanings. The rule for passive forms with

      active meanings holds except for certain forms among the ....

      and the .... The participles with active forms

      are the .... and the .... The

      infinitive with an active form is the .... The

      participle with a passive form and a passive meaning is the

      ....

   2. Using the verb LOQUĪ, complete the following chart underlining each
      form in English or Latin which does not follow the basic rule for
      deponent verbs:

Participles

	Active Forms in Latin		Passive Forms in Latin	
	Latin	English	Latin	English
Present	....	....	....	....
Perfect	....	....	....	....
Future	....	....	....	....

3. Using the verb ŪTOR complete the following chart underlining each form in English or Latin which does not follow the basic rule for deponent verbs:

Infinitives

	Active Forms in Latin		Passive Forms in Latin	
	Latin	English	Latin	English
Present	....	....	....	....
Perfect	....	....	....	....
Future	....	....	....	....

4. Using the verb CŌNĀRĪ, complete the following in the second person singular only.

Indicative

	Latin	English
Present	....	....
Future	....	....
Imperfect	....	....
Perfect	....	....
Future perfect	....	....
Pluperfect	....	....

Subjunctive

	Latin	English
Present	....	⌊The English translation
Imperfect	....	depends on the use of the
Perfect	....	Latin subjunctive in a
Pluperfect	....	given sentence⌋

5. Using the verb ĒGREDĪ, complete the following:

<u>Imperative</u>

	Latin	English
Present	Singular	....
	Plural	....

6. Semi-deponent verbs are so-called because they are ....

in the present system and .... in the perfect system.

7. Certain deponent verbs govern the .... case rather

than the .... case for the English direct object

because they are really .... verbs.

CHAPTER XXXIV

NAME _____ SECTION _____ DATE _____

II. DRILL.

A. Label the subjunctive forms by person, number and tense and translate the remaining forms.

a. ūsūrum esse

....

k. ūtātūr

....

b. patiēris

....

l. passum esse

....

c. ūsus esset

....

m. ūtētur

....

d. pateris

....

n. patientēs

....

e. ūsus

....

o. patiendus est

....

f. patere

....

p. patiātur

....

g. ūterētur

....

q. patitur

....

h. patī

....

r. patiēmur

....

i. ūtitur

....

s. arbitrārētur

....

j. passī sunt

....

t. arbitrētur

....

B. Supply the correct form for the verbs in parentheses and translate.

a. Ad īnsulam .... (proficīscī, 1st person plural, future).

....

b. Aquā ....(ūtī, 3rd person plural, perfect).

....

c. Puellās servāre ....(cōnārī, lst person singular,

imperfect). ....

d. In exsilium eum ....(sequī, 3rd person plural, pluper-

fect). ....

e. Mala eīs ....(patī, future passive participle) sunt.

....

C. Translate the following.

a. About to die, he dared to speak.

....

b. We often used the island to preserve our safety.

....

c. Having started from the city, they followed the enemy.

....

d. They enjoy the water and fruits of that island.

....

e. His son was born that night at a friend's house.

....

III. PRACTICE SENTENCES. (Before translating each, read the Latin _aloud_ twice.)

a. Arbitrātur haec mala patienda esse. ....

....

b. Cōnābimur haec mala patī. ....

....

c. Nisi morī vīs, patere haec mala. ....

....

d. Maxima mala passus, homō miser mortuus est. ....

....

e. Hīs verbīs dictīs, eum sequī ausī sumus. ....

....

f. Haec verba locūtī, profectī sumus nē in eō locō miserō morerēmur. ...

....

....

g. Sī quis vīnō eius generis ūtī audeat, celeriter moriātur. ....

....

h. Eōdem diē fīlius eius nātus est et mortuus est. ....

....

i. Omnibus opibus nostrīs ūtāmur ut patria nostra servētur. ....

....

j. Sī melioribus librīs ūsī essent, plūra didicissent. ....

....

CHAPTER XXXV

Dative with Special Verbs; Dative with Compounds.

OBJECTIVES:

1. To become familiar with Latin special verbs which govern the dative case.

2. To become familiar with Latin compound verbs which govern the dative case.

I. GRAMMAR.
   /REPEAT ALOUD A NUMBER OF TIMES THE EXAMPLES OF SPECIAL VERBS WHICH TAKE THE DATIVE OF INDIRECT OBJECT: CREDO TIBI, IGNOSCO TIBI, ETC. (W. pp. 168-169)/.

   1. Certain special verbs in Latin govern the .... case rather than the .... case for the English direct object.

   2. There is no satisfactory rule for knowing which Latin verbs are in the above category. Two clues for spotting them involve writing those having an English translation which includes the preposition .... and memorizing a sample .... or .... in the .... case after the verb.

   3. One possible guide to the use of the dative with certain compound Latin verbs is that, when the simple verb (which does not itself normally take the dative) can be substituted for the compound verb, the dative case /is or is not/ .... likely to be used; and that, when the .... or the .... has by its own meaning added a special new meaning to the simple verb, the resultant compound verb may take the .... case.

CHAPTER XXXV

NAME _____ SECTION _____ DATE _____

II. DRILL.

A. After writing the Latin for HIM and/or IT (from IS, EA, ID), in the correct case, after the following, translate the expression.

a. cognōscunt ....

b. ignōscunt ....

c. serviunt ....

d. servant ....

e. patiuntur ....

f. invenient ....

g. nocent ....

h. placent ....

i. iaciunt ....

j. crēdunt ....

k. carent ....

l. hortantur ....

m. sequuntur ....

n. persuādent ....

o. ūtuntur ....

B. Supply the correct form for the words in parentheses and translate.

a. ....(lēx, object idea) comprehendō.

....

b. ....(rēs pūblica, object idea) nocuērunt.

....

c. ....(exercitus) ūsī sumus.

....

d. ....(servus, plural, object idea) imperāvī.

....

e. Praemium ....(ego, object idea) placet.

....

C. Translate the following.

a. Let us obey the law.

....

b. The guards served him well.

....

c. They persuaded the author.

....

d. The army spared no resources.

....

e. A father forgives his son.

....

III. PRACTICE SENTENCES. (Before translating each, read the Latin _aloud_ twice.)

a. Servī aliīs hominibus serviunt. ....

b. Ille servus fīliō meō servīvit et eum servāvit. ....

....

c. Sī quis hunc labōrem suscēpisset, multōs servāvisset. ....

....

d. Sī Deum nōbīs ignōscere volumus, nōs dēbēmus aliīs hominibus ignōscere.

....

e. Mihi nunc nōn crēdunt, neque umquam fīliō meō crēdere volent. ....

....

f. Cum bonā fidē carērēs, tibi crēdere nōn poterant. ....

....

g. Huic ducī pāreāmus ut nōbīs parcat et urbem servet. ....

....

h. Nisi Caesar cīvibus placēbit, vītae eius nōn parcent. ....

....

i. Vēritātī et sapientiae semper studeāmus et pāreāmus. ....

....

j. Optimīs rēbus semper studēte sī vērē esse fēlīcēs vultis. ....

....

CHAPTER XXXVI

Jussive Noun Clauses;
FĪŌ.

OBJECTIVES:

1. To review Latin indirect discourse, i.e. indirect statement (Chapter XXV) and indirect question (Chapter XXX).

2. To review direct commands, i.e. imperative and jussive subjunctive (Chapter XXVIII) and to learn how an indirect command is expressed in Latin by a jussive noun clause.

3. To review regular adverbial clauses of purpose (Chapter XXVIII) since the jussive noun clause is in form identical with the purpose clause, although in use it is a noun (or substantive) clause employed as the direct object of a verb of command.

4. To learn the use of FIERĪ as a special passive form for the verb FACERE.

I. GRAMMAR.
   (MEMORIZE PARADIGMS AND VOCABULARY BY REPEATING THEM ALOUD!)

   1. That feature of a language which repeats a statement, question or

      command rather than express it directly is called ....

      ....

   2. Latin verbs of saying, knowing, thinking and perceiving are often

      followed by a subordinate clause of ....

      whose verb is in the .... mood. The subject of

      these clauses is not in the .... case but in the

      .... case. English clauses of this type are intro-

      duced by the conjunction ....

   3. Latin verbs of asking, saying, knowing and perceiving are often

      followed by a subordinate clause of ....

      whose verb is in the .... mood. In Latin and in

      English, clauses of this type are introduced by an ....

      word.

4. Direct commands are rendered in Latin in the first person by the

    ...., in the second person by

    the .... and in the third person by the ....

    ....

5. An indirect command is usually rendered in English by an ....

    clause but in Latin by a ....

    clause which is similar to an adverbial clause of ....

    However, since indirect commands are objects of verbs of command, they

    are not adverbial clauses but are .... clauses.

    Both are introduced in Latin by the conjunctions ....

    for the positive and .... for the negative, and the verbs in

    both these clauses are in the .... mood.

6. List six Latin verbs of command or request which can be followed by

    a noun clause of indirect command: ...., ...

    ...., ..., ..., and

    ....

CHAPTER XXXVI

NAME _____ SECTION _____ DATE _____

II. DRILL.

A. Label the subjunctives by person, number and tense and translate the
   remaining forms.

a. faciendus   k. fīet

....

b. fīāmus   l. fit

....

c. fīent   m. fīat

....

d. fierem   n. fierētis

....

e. fīant   o. fierī

....

f. fīunt   p. factī sīmus

....

g. fīēbāmus   q. faciam

....

h. fīēs   r. fēcimus

....

i. factus esse   s. factus essēs

....

j. fierent   t. facta eris

....

B. Supply the correct form for the verbs in parentheses and translate.

a. Eīs persuāsimus nē eī .... (nocēre, 3rd person plural).

....

b. Eōs hortor ut .... (accēdere, 3rd person plural).

....

c. Ab eā quaesīveram ut mihi .... (ignōscere, 3rd

person singular). ....

d. Imperāvit eī nē potentior ....(fierī, 3rd person sin-

gular). ....

e. Monēsne mē ut tibi ....(parēre, 1st person singular)?

....

C. Translate the following.

a. Persuade him to become the leader.

....

b. Warn him not to have fear.

....

c. They ordered (use imperō) him to accept the prize.

....

d. The woman begged her daughter not to depart.

....

e. We urged them to confess the plot without fear.

....

III. PRACTICE SENTENCES. (Before translating each, read the Latin aloud twice.)

a. Dīxit eōs litterīs Latīnīs studēre. ....

....

b. Dīxit cūr litterīs Latīnīs studērent. ....

....

c. Dīxit ut litterīs Latīnīs studērent. ....

....

d. Tē rogō cūr hoc fēcerīs. ....

e. Tē rogō ut hoc faciās. ....

f. Ā tē petō ut pāx fīat. ....

g. Ā mē petēbant nē bellum facerem. ....

....

h. Eum ōrāvī nē rēgī turpī pārēret. ....

....

i. Vōs ōrāmus ut discipulī ācerrimī fīātis. ....

....

j. Cūrāte ut hoc faciātis. ....

CHAPTER XXXVII

Conjugation of EŌ;
Constructions of Place and Time.

OBJECTIVES:

1. To learn the conjugational peculiarities of the irregular verb ĪRE in the active voice only (passive rare).

2. To review the syntax of regular Latin place constructions with prepositions.

3. To learn the special Latin place constructions for names of cities and towns and for DOMUS. This necessarily involves learning the locative case.

4. To review the ablative of time which was covered in Chapter XV, and to learn the use of the accusative to indicate duration of time (time how long).

I. GRAMMAR.
(MEMORIZE PARADIGMS AND VOCABULARY BY REPEATING THEM ALOUD!)

1. Analysis of the present infinitive of the Latin irregular verb ĪRE

shows that its normal stem is simply the letter ....

The irregularity of the verb derives from the fact that this stem

vowel becomes .... before the initial vowel of endings

beginning with ...., ..., and ....

The only conjugated forms thus affected then are two persons of the

.... indicative and all six persons of the

.... subjunctive. Other forms affected are the

declined .... and the ....

(which we shall study in Chapter XXXIX).

2. The future of this fourth conjugation verb (is or is not)............

regularly formed and has the future endings found in (Name one.) cōgō,

cūrō, fīō ....

3. Complete the following summary of the syntax of regular Latin
    expressions of place:

	Preposition(s)	Case
a. from which	....	....
b. where	....	....
c. to which	....	....

4. With names of cities/towns, the Romans used the special locative case,
    whose forms coincide with other familiar declensional forms as follows:

	Singular	Plural
a. Declension 1	....	....
b. Declension 2	....	....
c. Declension 3	....	....

5. Complete the following summary of the syntax of special Latin expres-
    sions of place involving names of cities or towns.

	Preposition(s)	Case
a. where	....	....
b. from which	....	....
c. to which	....	....

6. Complete the following summary of the syntax of Latin expressions of
    time:

	Preposition(s)	Case
a. when	....	....
b. within which	....	....
c. how long	....	....

CHAPTER XXXVII

NAME _____ SECTION _____ DATE _____

II. DRILL.

  A. Label the subjunctive by person, number and tense and translate the
      remaining forms.

      a. iimus ....   f. ībāmus ....

      b. īrēmus ....   g. itūrus esse ....

      c. īssēmus ....   h. euntem ....

      d. eāmus ....   i. eunt ....

      e. iērunt ....   j. ībunt ....

  B. Translate the following.

      a. ūnum diem ....   g. domum ....

      b. ūnō diē ....   h. Athēnīs ....

      c. Rōmae ....   i. domī ....

      d. multōs diēs ....   j. Athēnās ....

      e. Rōmam ....   k. domō ....

      f. in navem ....   l. in nave ....

  C. Supply the correct form of the word in parentheses and translate.

      a. Frāter meus ....(Athēnae) abiit.

      ....

      b. ....(Rōma) it.

      ....

      c. ....(domus) abierat.

      ....

      d. Deinde, ...(Athēnae) rediit.

      ....

      e. Dēnique, ...(domus) pereāmus.

      ....

D.   Translate the following:

    a.   My friends left home within one hour.

    ....

    b.   They will remain in Rome for a few days.

    ....

    c.   Let us return to Athens in one day.

    ....

    d.   He will go to the island on that day.

    ....

    e.   One may say that they returned rapidly.

    ....

III.   PRACTICE SENTENCES.   (Before translating each, read the Latin _aloud_ twice.)

    a.   Paucīs hōrīs Rōmam ībimus. ....

    b.   Nōs ad urbem īmus; illī domum eunt. ....

    ....

    c.   Cūr domō tam celeriter abīstī? ....

    d.   Rōmam veniunt ut cum frātre meō Athēnās eant. ....

    ....

    e.   Ad mortem hāc ex urbe abī et perī nē ego peream. ....

    ....

    f.   Frātre tuō Rōmae interfectō, Athēnās rediērunt. ....

    ....

    g.   Negāvit sē velle in istā terrā multōs diēs remanēre. ....

    ....

    h.   Dīxistī tē domum Athēnīs ūnā hōrā reditūrum esse. ....

    ....

i. Eīs diēbus solitī sumus Athēnīs esse. ....

....

j. Sī amīcīs eius Rōmae nocuissent, Rōmam brevissimō tempore redīsset. .

....

....

CHAPTER XXXVIII

Relative Clauses of Characteristic;
Dative of Reference.

OBJECTIVES:

1. To review the declension of relative pronouns (already learned in Chapter XVII).

2. To review regular Latin relative clauses (also learned in Chapter XVII) which state a fact about the antecedent and whose verb is, therefore, in the indicative mood.

3. To review the six types, learned thus far, of Latin subordinate clauses which require the subjunctive (See Chapters XXVIII, XXIX, XXX, XXXI, XXXIII and XXXVI).

4. To learn the use of the subjunctive in relative clauses of characteristic.

5. To learn the use of the dative of reference, or interest, in Latin.

I. GRAMMAR.
(MEMORIZE PARADIGMS AND VOCABULARY BY REPEATING THEM ALOUD!)

1. The verb in regular Latin relative clauses is in the indicative mood because the clause expresses a .... about the antecedent.

2. Complete the following by inserting the proper forms of the Latin relative pronoun.

	Singular			Plural		
	M	F	N	M	F	N
Nom	....	....	....	....	....	....
Gen	....	....	....	....	....	....
Dat	....	....	....	....	....	....
Acc	....	....	....	....	....	....
Abl	....	....	....	....	....	....

3. The six types of Latin subordinate clauses already learned which require the subjunctive mood are:

   a. .... d. ....

   b. .... e. ....

   c. .... f. ....

4. Another type of Latin subordinate clause requiring the subjunctive

   mood consists of relative clauses which state a ....

   of an antecedent which is ...., ...,

   ...., or ....

5. Translate the following Latin main clauses which are typical of those usually preceding a relative clause of characteristic:

   a. Sunt quī. ....

   b. Sunt quae. ....

   c. Quis est quī? ....

   d. Quid est quod? ....

   e. Nēmō est quī. ....

   f. Nihil est quod. ....

   g. Sōlus est quī. ....

6. The regular Latin dative of indirect object is considered to be

   .... to the verb and thus might be called the

   .... or .... dative. Conversely,

   the dative of reference, or interest, is not so essential to the

   .... but is included in a sentence for an

   ....

7. Give three possible translations of TIBI used in the following Latin sentence as a dative of reference or interest: Domum redīre tibi dēbēmus?

   a. ....?

b. ....?

c. ....?

CHAPTER XXXVIII

II. DRILL.

  A. Supply the correct form of the verb in parentheses and translate.

      a. Sola est quae odium ....(sentīre, present).

      ....

      b. Quis est cuius fātum certum ....(esse, present)?

      ....

      c. Puella quae opus ....(facere, present) ibi est.

      ....

      d. Tibi nemo erat quī odiō ....(cōnsūmere, passive,

      imperfect). ....

      e. Frāter meus quī mē ....(amāre, present) mē dēfendet.

      ....

  B. Translate the following.

      a. There are people who do not hesitate to forgive.

      ....

      b. There are few who do not dread pain.

      ....

      c. Who is there who doubts his authority?

      ....

      d. The citizens who doubted his authority were sent away.

      ....

      e. They were the only ones who used their feet.

      ....

III. PRACTICE SENTENCES. (Before translating each, read the Latin <u>aloud</u> twice.)

   a. At nēmō erat quī istum hominem turpem dēfenderet. ....

   ....

   b. Quid est quod virī plūs metuant quam tyrannum? ....

   ....

   c. Quis est quī inter lībertātem et imperium tyrannī dubitet? ....

   ....

   d. Rōmae antīquae erant quī pecūniam plūs quam rem pūblicam amārent. ....

   ....

   ....

   e. Quis est quī tantum dolōrem ferre possit? ....

   ....

   f. Nihil sciō quod mihi facilius esse possit. ....

   ....

   g. Ducem quaerō quem omnēs laudent. ....

   ....

   h. Illum ducem magnum quaerō quem omnēs laudant. ....

   ....

   i. Virīs antīquīs nihil erat quod melius esset quam virtūs et sapientia.

   ....

   ....

   j. Nihil metuendum est quod animō nocēre nōn possit. ....

   ....

CHAPTER XXXIX

Gerund and Gerundive.

OBECTIVES:

1. To review the Latin future passive participle, or gerundive, learned in Chapter XXIV.

2. To learn the declension of the Latin verbal noun or gerund.

3. To learn the gerund and gerundive constructions used by the Romans.

I. GRAMMAR.
(MEMORIZE PARADIGMS AND VOCABULARY BY REPEATING THEM ALOUD!)

1. The Latin gerundive is a .... which may be modified like a .... and is used as an ....

2. The Latin gerundive is declined like an .... of the .... declension.

3. The Latin gerund is a .... which may be modified like a .... and is used as a ....

4. In view of this, the gerund is declined as a .... of the .... declension in the oblique cases of the singular of the .... gender. The .... of the verb serves as the nominative.

5. The Latin gerund, using VĪVERE, is declined as follows:

	Latin	English
Nom	....	....
Gen	....	....

Latin	English
Dat	....
Acc	....
Abl	....

6. Give an English translation of each of the following sentences and
    underline the Latin structure which the Romans preferred:

    a. Discimus legendō librōs cum curā. ....

    ....

    b. Discimus librīs legendīs cum curā. ....

    ....

CHAPTER XXXIX

NAME _____ SECTION _____ DATE _____

II. DRILL.

A. Identify the following verb forms as gerunds or gerundives.

    a. operibus faciendīs.   ....

    b. dēlendī causā   ....

    c. iniūriam oppugnandam   ....

    d. audiendō vōcem   ....

    e. cognōscendī lēgem   ....

    f. aedificiōrum dēlendōrum   ....

    g. lēgis cognōscendae   ....

    h. oppugnandum iniūriam   ....

    i. vōce audiendā   ....

    j. spēs vivendi   ....

B. Supply the correct form of the verbs in parentheses and translate.

    a. Aedificiī ....(vidēre, gerundive) cupidī erāmus.

    ....

    b. Ars ....(scrībere, gerund) laudābātur.

    ....

    c. Hoc dictum est contrā versūs ....(scrībere, gerun-

    dive). ....

    d. Ad pācem ....(petere, gerundive) venient.

    ....

    e. Timor .... (īre, gerund) domum vērus erat.

    ....

C. Translate the following.

    a. We came for the sake of hearing your voice. (gerundive)

    ....

    b. Reading is necessary. ('gerund' – See W. p. 187 n. 3)

    ....

    c. They saw him after reading the letter. (gerundive)

    ....

    d. By reading we become wise. (gerund)

    ....

    e. He spoke in favor of (prō) freeing the city. (gerundive)

    ....

III. PRACTICE SENTENCES. (Before translating each, read the Latin _aloud_ twice.)

    a. Experiendō discimus. ....

    b. Sē discendō dedit. ....

    c. Discendī causā ad lūdum tuum vēnērunt. ....

    ....

    d. Metus moriendī eum terrēbat. ....

    e. Spēs vīvendī post mortem multōs hortātur. ....

    ....

    f. Cōgitandō eōs superāvit. ....

    g. Sē dedit litterīs Latīnīs discendīs. ....

    ....

    h. Librum scrīpsit dē lībertāte dēfendendā. ....

    ....

    i. Sapientiōrēs fīmus vītā experiendā. ....

    ....

    j. Multum tempus cōnsūmpsit in hīs operibus faciendīs. ....

    ....

CHAPTER XL

Numerals;
Genitive of the Whole.

OBJECTIVES:

1. To learn the peculiarities of Latin cardinal and ordinal numerals.

2. To learn the use of the Latin genitive of the whole, or partitive
    genitive.

I. GRAMMAR.
    (MEMORIZE PARADIGMS AND VOCABULARY BY REPEATING THEM ALOUD!)

    1. When a Latin partitive word (i.e. one indicating a part of a whole)

        is accompanied by a word indicating the whole, the word indicating

        the whole is put in the .... case. The construction

        is called the .... of the .... or

        ....

    2. The genitive of the whole is often encountered in Latin with the

        neuter nominative and accusative of certain .... or

        ....

    3. The genitive of the whole may itself be the neuter singular of a

        .... declension ....

    4. Latin cardinal numerals from .... through ....

        and the word .... meaning one thousand are ....

        adjectives.

    5. The Latin cardinal numerals ...., ..., and

        ...., as well as the hundreds from .... through

        .... are .... adjectives.

6. The Latin word for the plural 'thousands' is .... It
    is an .... of the ....
    declension. It is followed by the .... of the ....
    .... when there is need to express the idea of the whole.

7. All cardinal numerals other than MĪLIA and the word ....
    are followed by the prepositions .... or .... and
    the .... case when it is necessary to express the
    idea of the whole.

8. Latin ordinal numbers are declinable adjectives of the ....
    and .... declensions.

9. Decline the Latin cardinal numerals two and three. (Plural only
    for obvious reason).

	TWO			THREE		
	M	F	N	M	F	N
Nom	....	....	....	....	....	....
Gen	....	....	....	....	....	....
Dat	....	....	....	....	....	....
Acc	....	....	....	....	....	....
Abl	....	....	....	....	....	....

10. The genitive of ūnus, -a, -um is ....
    and the dative is ....

CHAPTER XL

NAME _____ SECTION _____ DATE _____

II. DRILL.

    A. Translate the following.

        a. decem cīvēs   ....

        b. trēs ex sex cīvibus ....

        c. centum cīvēs   ....

        d. centum ex cīvibus   ....

        e. tria mīlia cīvium   ....

        f. quīdam ex cīvibus ....

        g. quid speī?   ....

        h. minus metūs   ....

        i. nihil aquae   ....

        j. satis auxiliī   ....

    B. Supply the correct form of the nouns in parentheses and translate.

        a. Mīlle ....(vōx, plural) audientur.

    ....

        b. Multa mīlia ....(vōx, plural) audientur.

    ....

        c. ....(duo) capita non habēmus.

    ....

        d. ....(tertius) hominem reperient.

    ....

        e. Post ....(septem) annōs, rediērunt.

    ....

C. Translate the following.

    a. Four of the slaves served three masters.

....

    b. One of the masters knows.

....

    c. It is necessary to send a thousand men.

....

    d. The author wrote fourteen verses.

....

    e. I read the fourteenth verse.

....

III. PRACTICE SENTENCES. (Before translating each, read the Latin <u>aloud</u> twice.)

    a. Salvē, mī amīce. Quid agis? Quid novī est? ....

....

    b. Salvē et tū. Bene. Nihil novī. ....

....

    c. Vīsne audīre aliquid bonī? Satis dīvitiārum dēnique accēpī! ....

....

    d. At quid bonī est in dīvitiīs sōlīs? Satisne etiam sapientiae habēs?

....

    e. Plūrimī autem virī dīvitēs multum metūs sentiunt. ....

....

    f. Pauperēs saepe sunt fēlīciōrēs et minus metūs habent. ....

....

    g. Novem ex ducibus nōs hortātī sunt ut plūs auxiliī praestārēmus. .....

....

h. Numquam satis ōtiī habēbit; at aliquid ōtiī melius est quam nihil. ..

....

i. Nostrīs temporibus omnēs plūs metūs et minus speī habēmus. ....

....

j. Magna fidēs et virtūs omnibus virīs reperiendae sunt. ....

....